Managing Your Union-Free Workforce

A CLV Special Report

Managing Your Union-Free Workforce

A CLV Special Report

Jamie Knight

CARSWELL

A THOMSON COMPANY

National Library of Canada Cataloguing in Publication

Knight, Jamie
    Managing your union-free workforce / Jamie Knight.

(A CLV special report)
ISBN 0-459-27731-6

    1. Personnel management. 2. Open and closed shop. 3. Labor laws and legislation—Ontario. I. Title. II. Series: CLV special report series

HF5549.K55 2002   658.3   C2002-903934-7

CARSWELL

A THOMSON COMPANY

One Corporate Plaza, 2075 Kennedy Road, Toronto, Ontario M1T 3V4
Customer Relations:
Toronto 1-416-609-3800
Elsewhere in Canada/U.S. 1-800-387-5162
Fax 1-416-298-5094

Brief Contents

Contents

CONTENTS

CONTENTS

Acknowledgments

Good human resources management is built on personal relationships. To be effective, you should be interested in people — all sorts of people. You should like people. You should expect a great deal from people and from yourself. When your expectations are met, you should celebrate, then expect even more. In this way, effective human resources management also builds personal relationships.

As a professional working in human resources, I have a strong belief that people are special. Each person is unique. Certainly, there are standards to set and procedures to follow, but there are no cookie cutters. Every day is full of new challenges. Every person with whom we work has the potential to wow us and test us in new and marvellous ways, or at least ways that cause us to marvel. No solution that we achieve today will govern all of our tomorrows.

Personal relationships are both the root and the flower of good human resources management. With that in mind, I want to open this book with some comments about my background, my career and some important people I have met along the way. I trust that they will help to illustrate some of the points that will be made throughout the book.

I went to law school without much idea of what would happen afterwards. After two years of under-achievement, I took a year off and went to Europe with my girlfriend. Betty was still my girlfriend when we returned seven months later, so we got married. It was five months before law school started again and I needed a job. By blind luck, I was available about a month ahead of the other university students, who were still in the midst of writing exams. I was hired by what was then called the Toronto General Hospital. Essentially my job was to hire the other university students to summer positions as soon as their exams ended. That is how I started my career in human resources. It was 1981.

There is no substitute for luck, and mine was to continue. I secured an articling position with one of the premier boutique labour law firms in Ontario, Mathews, Dinsdale & Clark. I am no longer there, but the firm's high reputation has been unscarred by my early departure. In between articles and working as an associate with MDC, I worked for a couple of years in-house with Versa Services, now known as Aramark Canada. As a young labour lawyer, Versa was a terrific place to start. They had food service and cleaning contracts all over the place, all across Canada. I was always negotiating collective agreements or acting in arbitration cases, and Versa dealt with just about every union you could think of. In the process, I got to discover Canada and very small planes.

Since 1988, I have benefited from the wisdom and support of my colleagues in the law firm once known as Fraser & Beatty, now called Fraser Milner Casgrain LLP. FMC is a leading National Business Law firm, with a wonderful group of employment and labour lawyers, not only in Toronto, but also in five other offices, from Montreal to Vancouver. At present, we have 15 labour and employment lawyers in Toronto and some 40 labour and employment lawyers in our offices across Canada.

I have met some fine people in my 20 years in human resources — including lawyers, arbitrators, managers, employees, public servants and union representatives. It is always risky to name names, because there are always others who could have been named and I will apologize in advance to those I leave out. That said, there are six people who I have singled out for special mention. I hope they won't mind.

First, I want to acknowledge my parents, Ed and Margie Knight. They are now both retired, although thankfully healthy and very active. My father was a school principal for many years. What impressed me most was how much Dad was admired and appreciated by his staff. He challenged his people to achieve excellence and to pursue the objectives of their profession, which was to teach their brains out and to open up the world to the students with whom they had been entrusted.

My mother taught me her own lesson, from which all of us can learn. After choosing to devote many years to raising four children, Mom went back to school, completed her degree and became qualified in the very specialized area of teaching children with learning disabilities. Living in Canada in the 21st century, most of us are blessed with good health and long careers. It is never too late to take on new challenges and to excel in areas that are of great importance to the communities in which we live.

At Versa Services, I had a boss who was larger than life, a real character. Some of you reading this may know Phil Coupey. I had more good luck — I got to work for Phil before I knew much of anything. Phil taught me two of the most valuable lessons that I have learned. The first lesson occurred in my first week of work. We had a grievance to deal with in one of our locations. Who can remember what it was about, it doesn't matter. What matters is that I researched the heck out of this problem and very proudly showed up in Phil's office with a ten-page memorandum, including footnotes. Phil threw it in the garbage and said something like this: "First, I only read one page, maybe two if I am really interested. Second, I know that you went to law school, you don't have to prove it to me, just tell me what you think we should do."

The second lesson happened during my first set of collective agreement negotiations. I had all of my creative engines firing. In those days, we did not have laptops to tap away at, but I madly scribbled proposals, counter-proposals, packages and alternatives on mounds of paper. I worked well into the wee hours of the morning and came out with a collective agreement that everyone thought was a pretty good resolution. Phil had come to watch me in action, but he went to bed at 10 p.m. The next day, when we were driving back to Toronto, with me crashed in the back seat, Phil asked me how I thought I had done. I said that I was pretty pleased with myself. Phil said that I worked too hard.

When you are involved in human resources, you should be patient. As a patient person, let other people do some work. Open up participation in the evolution of the ideas that eventually become resolutions. You cannot solve all of the problems all by yourself, even though you may be technically capable and sufficiently energetic to do just that. If you work too hard and if you try too hard to drag people kicking and screaming to a settlement, then your solution may have no more strength than the paper upon which it is written.

The fourth person is my law partner and good friend, Kristin Taylor. Kristin sometimes claims that I have taught her a few things along the way, but I have probably learned much more than I have taught. There are three lessons that Kristin has taught particularly well. The first is that employment lawyers (and all Human Resources Professionals "HRP's") are in a service business. The best advice in the world may be of little use unless it is also prompt. The second lesson is that there is no substitute for excellence. HRP's and employment lawyers are dealing with the most precious asset of any organization — people. In helping to create the finest workplaces we can and in maximizing the productivity of the workplaces for which we are responsible, we should strive to be excellent in our work and we should demand excellence in others. The third lesson is that people really matter. Everyone has the potential to contribute. Some have more potential than others and some use more of the potential that they have. Great results can come from the most unexpected places. Kristin never gives up on anyone until that person gives up. At some point an employment relationship has to end, but we often rush to that point with reckless energy, when we should be spending our time and efforts in helping someone find and use the potential that s/he has.

The fifth person on my list is no longer with us, but he remains a big part of me. Brent Snell was killed suddenly in June 2000. He was 42 and full of life. Brent was widely admired, and the many persons who knew him, even people who did not know him very well, have keenly felt his loss. Of his many attributes, there are two features of Brent that continue to guide me. First, he had a very good sense of what was right and he did not allow himself to be pulled off line when travelling the right course. Second, he listened very carefully to other people, so that they felt valuable and they felt that Brent valued them. Brent did not do this in any calculated manner; he was genuinely interested in all kinds of other people, most especially if they were very different from him. The effect was profound — people who are listened to, who feel valuable and who feel that another person values them are incredibly loyal to that person. Without even trying, Brent commanded great loyalty from a wide and varied group of people.

The sixth and final person I want to mention is the most pleasant person I know, my wife Betty. Everything that you need to know about dealing with other people you can learn from Betty. She is quick to praise good efforts, knowing that the results will follow. She does not hesitate to point out laziness and carelessness, knowing that the individual person is not fundamentally flawed. Most lazy and careless people have yet to meet the acceptable standard (whether it is picking up discarded clothes or writing an essay on folk heroes in children's literature). That is what managers and leaders are for, to set high standards and insist that the standards are met. Most of all, Betty takes great joy in all aspects of life; she recognizes that it is all an adventure. Open your eyes and see opportunity, even in the smallest actions. It is easy to find fault in each other, but there is so much more in each of us to appreciate and admire. It is from Betty that I have learned to look past the flaws that all of us have and focus instead on the virtues that are there to be found. Each member of your workplace can make positive contributions or they would not have been hired in the first place. A little effort and the right attitude may be all that is needed to bring positive contributions to the surface.

The observations and recommendations in the pages that follow come from twenty years of experience in human resources and in the practice of labour and employment law. I have been fortunate to teach with the University of Guelph, Office of Open Learning for the past twelve years. I have been involved with two recurring courses in particular: Labour and Employment Law, which is a course sanctioned by the Human Resources Professionals Association of Ontario and part of the CHRP program. The other course is a Supervisory Development Program that focuses on teaching front-line and second-line supervisors the essentials of management, including the legal aspects of human resources management. Many of the ideas in these pages come from those two courses and the enthusiastic participants whom I have met.

Many of the other ideas come from my partners and colleagues at my law firm, Fraser Milner Casgrain LLP, as well as my professional colleagues who specialize in labour and employment law, whether acting for employers, unions or individual employees. I have enjoyed the confidence of executives, managers and human resources professionals for a wide variety of clients over the years, as well as the union representatives who have sat on the other side of the table. To all of them, and to all of you, I extend my thanks.

Finally, I would like to express my appreciation and thanks to Derry McDonell of Carswell, who encouraged me to organize my thoughts in this book, and who remained patient while I did so.

In the usual way, although I have had many sources for ideas, any errors or instances of clumsy drafting are entirely my responsibility. I may well be asked to improve on my work in the future. Please feel free to send me your own thoughts, criticisms or examples. My e-mail address is jamie.knight@fmc-law.com. I cannot promise a response, but I can promise my interest in your views.

Jamie Knight
Port Credit, Ontario, May 2002

◆
INTRODUCTION

Good human resources management is an important key to the success of Canadian workplaces. In general terms, the objective of good human resources management is to balance the needs and goals of the different players in the workplace. The key human resources balance in a non-union workplace is between the personal aspirations and idiosyncrasies of the employees and the primary purpose for the organization, be it profit (private sector) or service (public sector).

A specific objective of good human resources management in a non-union workplace is to remain non-union. Achieving and maintaining a balanced workplace is entirely consistent with the important objective of staying non-union. In fact, the best chance an organization has of avoiding unionization is through the application of excellent principles of human resources management.

Lessons from Union Workplaces

In the pages that follow, a major theme is that non-union workplaces can improve their human resources management by studying unionized workplaces. It is certainly unhealthy to manage in a perpetual state of crisis, driven at all times by a fear of union organizing; however it is useful to maintain a healthy respect for the possibility that your workers could choose to be unionized. The best way to avoid this possibility is for management to understand the union's sales pitch and its bargaining objectives. Then, to the extent possible, and always in a manner consistent with the objectives of the organization, management should try to replicate much of what the union would promise to employees in an organizing drive. It is difficult for a union to sell something that already has been provided by management.

In managing human resources, with the objective of avoiding unionization, non-union workplaces have important lessons to learn from union workplaces. It is not simply a matter of copying what is done in a union workplace. Each workplace is unique, with its own history and culture. Non-union workplaces have some significant advantages for employers. These advantages are derived from the fact

1

that the restrictions of a collective agreement are absent, as is the possibility of third-party intervention into workplace disputes. In replicating what is done in a union workplace, a non-union employer should do so only to the extent and in the fashion that seems comfortable, both for management and for the employees.

It should also be made plain that success cannot be found simply by doing the opposite of what a union employer is required to do because of its union relationship. In fact, that would be a very poor approach. Many union workplaces provide a structure that is useful, both in general and in respect of many of the component parts. At the very least, this structure should be understood. As the non-union workplace builds its framework of good human resources management, the framework of union workplaces can provide a very helpful reference point.

I should be clear that it is not the intention of this book to focus on tactics to use in responding to union organizing campaigns. For one thing, the rules of union organizing are quite particular and differ in each of the provincial jurisdictions and in the federal jurisdiction. For another thing, my focus is not on the narrow and specific hothouse activity of union organizing. Instead, I am concerned with establishing a framework for managing your human resources in a relatively stable workplace environment and in the long-term. In this respect, I am working from a foundation that is based on three assumptions:

- if you are using this book, you are probably working in a non-union workplace;
- if you are a member of management or a human resources professional ("HRP") in a non-union workplace, then you probably want your workplace to remain non-union and it is probably part of your job to help achieve that ongoing result; and
- it is undoubtedly also your goal and part of your job to operate the best workplace possible and to manage your human resources in a manner that helps them achieve their very best in conjunction with operational objectives.

The Importance of Good Human Resources Management

If the processes of employee relations are conducted effectively, the following results should be expected:

- management will be informed and knowledgeable, and committed to continuation of effective labour relations processes;
- plans to make changes in programs, technology, policies and procedures will take into consideration the perspectives of the employees and any employee representatives;
- operational objectives will be achieved with minimal conflict; people will work together on issues; operations will be efficient and effective in pursuit of objectives and in resolving issues;
- the different elements of the framework will be applied consistently and fairly;
- any complaint or suggestion will get a timely and effective response;
- employee morale will be high, which not only is more pleasant for everyone, but also fosters enhanced productivity; and
- there will be fewer requests for clarification of straightforward policies or terms and conditions of employment.

If, on the other hand, the processes of employee relations are ineffective, management may be exposed to the following risks:

- loss of productivity and service;
- inconsistent application of policies or terms of the phantom collective agreement (see page 37), resulting in low morale and increased costs;
- many complaints and few positive suggestions;
- escalation of conflict, which increases the risk of union organizing activity;
- too much management time spent dealing with employee relations issues at the expense of program issues;
- reactive and crisis-oriented relationships;
- over-reliance on third-party participation (public servants, adjudicators and the courts) to achieve the resolution of disputes.

Management must focus continuously on employee relations to ensure that employees work effectively and efficiently for the benefit of the organization. You should strive to manage all aspects of employee relations in a consistent and objective manner. Effective management will foster enhanced productivity, expeditious dispute resolution, good morale, and efficient communications. Achieving these objectives will depend upon the effective co-ordination of the interests of the workplace parties. With sensitivity, leadership and planning, these different interests can be satisfied with minimal conflict.

◆

CHAPTER 1

THE WORKPLACE PLAYERS

In a non-union workplace, the parties include workers, supervisors, higher-level management, professionals, confidential staff and third parties who are typically present in the workplace. There may also be employee organizations set up in a formal or informal manner, some involving management and others being entirely at the level of the workers. From a human resources standpoint, all of these players are necessary and must be suitably managed, directed, or at least acknowledged in order to carry out the objectives of the organization in an effective and efficient manner.

Before proceeding further, we should take a closer look at the players in the workplace.

Workers

In law, all sorts of people are employees, from casual workers right up to the president, who may also be the owner and majority shareholder. For our purposes, the term "workers" will be used to refer to subordinate employees, the so-called rank and file, who carry out instructions, but who do not typically instruct or direct other workers. It is these subordinate employees who are the potential targets of union organizers.

In a manufacturing plant, workers fall into two main groups, white collar or blue collar. These groupings are extremely important in the event of a union organizing drive, as we will discuss further, so they should not be ignored when it comes to the way in which management organizes the workplace. Workers in shipping and receiving, as well as drivers, are typically grouped with the blue-collar workers, while sales are grouped with the white collars. Laboratory, quality control, and technical staff may be blue or white depending on the precise nature and location of their work. Workers include lead hands or group leaders and sometimes even working managers, depending on how much authority is actually given to such leading employees.

In an office setting, workers are typically all in one employee group, no matter how many different classifications there may be. In certain specialized sectors, like health care, workers may be considered to be in different groupings, depending on the nature of their work. For example, nurses are grouped separately from other workers, sometimes even when those other workers have extensive overlap with nurses in terms of the jobs actually performed.

Workers can be part-time or full-time, regularly scheduled or on call. They can be short-term employees or "lifers". Student employees are workers. Workers can have specific contracts of employment, written or oral, with or without a defined duration, or they can simply be employed on a handshake or a nod. Some workers will have been around so long, that nobody can remember the terms and conditions of hire, if there were any.

To the surprise of many organizations, workers may also include contract personnel or even agency workers. It is one thing to bring in an agency employee for a few days or even a few weeks. It can become quite another thing when the agency employee stays around for several weeks or even months, even if on a part-time and casual basis. The employment relationship is not determined by who is signing the wage cheques. What is fundamental to the determination is who is in control. The party in control is typically the party that schedules and directly supervises the work. After the first couple of weeks (if not the first couple of hours), it is usually the party that is in control of where the work is being performed that is in control of the worker.

Lead Hands or Group Leaders

Especially in a production plant, it is common to have certain workers used as leaders of a work group, line or shift. These workers, who often have a special level of experience or expertise, fall below the level of supervisor, because they do not perform traditional management functions, as will be discussed immediately below. For the most part, they co-ordinate the flow of work, help to schedule production, and are instrumental in on-the-job-training. It is typical for lead hands to have a wide knowledge of many jobs in the plant, so they can fill in, either to replace missing workers, or as may be required to fulfill the needs of production. In a shift operation, especially in a smaller plant, lead hands may be the most senior employee on site during night and weekend shifts. In such cases, the lead hand would be considered to be a supervisor for the purposes of health and safety legislation, and would naturally take on many supervisory duties for the purposes of performance management.

Skilled Employees and Professional Workers

Skilled employees, such as electricians, millwrights, tool and die makers and licensed mechanics, are typically included in the group of workers in a manufacturing plant. Certainly in terms of what is a target group for the purposes of union organizing, skilled employees would be included in the blue collar bargaining unit. Other non-managerial employees are less likely to fit easily with either the blue collar or white-collar group of workers. They will be either in between, in something of a grey zone, or more clearly separate. These professional workers include quality specialists, laboratory technicians, engineers and computer programmers and technicians.

Depending on the nature of the service business or office environment, there may also be distinct groupings of professionals in a non-manufacturing setting. These employees are not managers, but they have unique and advanced skills that separate them from other white-collar employees.

Front-Line Supervisors

Front-line supervisors have a job that is both difficult and vitally important for successful human resources management. An employee does not become a supervisor just because s/he has that title or because s/he gets a salary instead of an hourly wage. The key is whether or not the employee has economic power over other employees. The most obvious indications of economic power are whether the supervisor can directly hire and fire employees. A person who cannot hire or fire acting alone is still a supervisor if his or her recommendation carries significant weight with the ultimate decision-maker. Understand that the mere ability to make a recommendation is not sufficient. To be a supervisor, and therefore part of management, the recommendation must be an effective one. It will not always carry the day, but it will generally receive careful consideration by the ultimate decision-maker.

Another aspect of economic power that would indicate supervisory status is the responsibility to discipline, especially if discipline could involve unpaid time off, even if that is as basic as having the power to send an employee home in the middle of the shift. As well, a supervisor would typically make or participate in decisions about promotions, demotions, lay-offs and significant work assignments. A supervisor would also be able to grant paid time off, whether prior to the end of a shift or scheduling vacation or lieu time.

The importance of the front-line supervisor is that s/he is the one who is most directly responsible for ensuring the efficient and effective operation of the workplace on a day-to-day basis. The supervisor may have some hand in the formation of policies, procedures and rules. Through day-to-day practices, the front-line supervisor is sure to be much more prominent in the implementation and, especially, the ongoing application of policy. The supervisor is typically the member of management who has first-hand or, at least, the best second-hand information about key incidents that occur in the workplace. In any situations involving issues of fundamental policy, discipline, safety or human rights, it is usually the supervisor who will be the key witness for management.

The front-line supervisor is also the member of the management team who is closest to the non-managerial employees. In many cases, the supervisor will have been promoted from "the ranks" and will still be plugged into the network that was built up while s/he was one of the workers. Even if hired from outside the workplace, a supervisor will often have values and experiences that are much closer to the workers than other members of the management team. It is quite natural that the supervisor will feel the pull of conflicting loyalties. While this sometimes can be a frustration to more senior levels of management, it is very helpful in any situation of crisis, such as a union organizing campaign. It is fundamental to the successful operation of any workplace, especially one in crisis, to be able to rely on the two-way communication stream that is created by a trusted and accessible supervisor.

Of all the lessons in human resources management that could be taught to the senior members of the management team, the two most important are two sides of the same coin:

- Trust your supervisors, and provide them with the training and the tools necessary to be able to exercise discretion when required and to take effective action in support of the objectives of the management team.

- Although the decisions of a front-line supervisor should not be supported at all costs, the supervisor should be supported at all times. If you have problems with the performance of a supervisor, deal with those problems in confidence and without creating a scapegoat for disaffected workers. You should be vigilant at all times not to cut your supervisor off at the knees. A front-line supervisor's authority must be built up, layer by layer. Unsupportive decisions of senior management that rashly interfere with supervisory actions can slice through the authority of a supervisor in a moment, thereby creating significant and sometimes irreparable harm. The harm created is to the very person that you need to rely on to run part or all of the workplace on a day-to-day basis. Undercut your front-line supervisors, and you are undercutting all of management.

Higher Level Management

Even in organizations with very flat management structures, it is generally the case that you will have second and higher tiers of management. These people may be very involved with the workers and they may be in direct and frequent communication with them; however, they remain at least one step removed in terms of hierarchy, such that the day-to-day supervision of the work force is, or ought to be, directed through a front line supervisor.

A challenge for higher-level management is to create direct and meaningful bonds with the workers while, at the same time, respecting and reinforcing the primary human resources responsibilities of the supervisor. It is important that higher level management does not create an informal hierarchy that essentially serves to bypass the formal hierarchy, such that the decisions of a supervisor, at least in important situations, become easily revised or even contradicted.

Human Resources Professionals and other Professional Staff

There is an important decision that organizations should make about the role of Human Resources Professionals ("HRP's") in human resources management. This should not be an accidental decision, but a deliberate choice. Is human resources management to be the responsibility of your operational supervisors and managers, or is it the responsibility of the HRP's? In my view, there is only one good choice. Operational management has to be responsible to manage its own people. The role of HRP's is still very significant, but it is a role of support and guidance. Everything that is written in this book is based on that fundamental design of human resources management. The people who are ultimately responsible for the quality and quantity of the goods and services must manage the people who are producing the goods or providing the services.

It is for this reason that the operations management should be directly involved in policy development, even if that effort is co-ordinated and led by HRP's. Operations management must also be involved in a decisive role in such key human resources situations as hiring, promotions, staffing levels, performance appraisals, discipline and dismissals.

Other professionals who will likely have a significant support role to play in human resources management include those on the financial side of the organization — internal auditors, accountants, and controllers — as well as those on the mechanical and engineering side.

The keys for all who manage human resources, and for HRP's in particular, are first to know the objectives of your organization, then try to bring out the full potential of all the people with whom you work within the organization in ways that will maximize the achievement of the objectives.

Confidential Staff

In all workplaces there are likely to be non-managerial clerical or secretarial workers who have a separate and unique status by virtue of who directs their work and the nature of the work that they perform. Confidential staff members have normal access to personnel records and to key information about the business. Typically, confidential staff members work in the human resources area or for company executives or the senior management of a plant or office.

Third Parties

Many workplaces have third parties who are routinely on site, either on an indefinite basis, or for limited terms. In this respect, I do not include agency workers, who are essentially doing the same kind of work as workers who are directly employed. Rather, my reference is to third parties who have distinct roles to play in the workplace. They may be cleaners, security staff, or food service employees. They may be involved in construction, maintenance, equipment installation or situations of technological change. They may also be involved at higher levels of management, including such people as accountants, outside auditors, consultants, benefits brokers, pension managers, and lawyers who specialize in such areas of the law as employment, labour, human resources, health and safety, and pensions and benefits.

We usually think of third parties in terms of other companies. In a company with multiple plants and offices, third parties may also be workers, professionals or managerial employees from other plants or offices.

Many modern workplaces have taken to contracting out peripheral functions. As well, specialized short-term projects will often be carried out by teams of outside contractors or specialized teams that move from plant to plant or from office to office within a larger company.

Employee Organizations and Representatives

When a workplaces does not have that most obvious of employee organizations, a trade union, it is important for management to understand, promote and co-operate with the formal and less formal employee organizations that are active in the workplace. The organization that is most like a trade union is an employee association, which in its most formal state may negotiate something that legally is, or is very like, a collective agreement. An employee association may also represent employees in individual disputes with the employer.

If an employee association is formally recognized by the employer and if it negotiates terms and conditions of employment in an agreement that is legally ratified or approved by the workers who are represented by the association, then the employer may be able to avoid union organizing activity except during the limited open periods that are provided for in labour legislation. If the legal requirements are met, the employee association would have the same legal status as a trade union. As a note of caution, employers are not supposed to be involved in the creation, administration or ongoing support of an employee association. If the employees are not able to establish and maintain an association on their own, then the workplace will remain completely vulnerable to union organizing activity.

It should be pointed out that some employers have had excellent success with employee associations. Other employers have found, over time, that an employee association is not only on a legal par with a trade union, but it is for practical purposes the same thing. In other words, some employee associations can be as difficult for an employer to deal with as a regular trade union.

In addition to employee associations, there may be other less obvious organizations that primarily exist for a social or benevolent purpose. Even though these groups may be informal and may not have any involvement with the terms and conditions of employment, by their mere existence and operation they can still provide some degree of leadership and common purpose to a group of employees.

Separate from employee organizations, there are also employee representatives who naturally evolve or who are required by law in all but the smallest workplaces, at least for the purposes of health and safety, but often for other policy purposes as well. These representatives may be selected by the workers themselves or appointed by management, preferably with some worker input. Good employers will look for opportunities to create leadership among the workers, as well as to create teamwork between the workers and the other players in the workplace. Any time that input would be useful, from policy formation to work methods, management should reach out to include worker representatives. This will not only enrich decision making, but will also create natural bonds that may become very useful in resisting union organizing activity.

◆

CHAPTER 2

THE BOUNDARIES OF HUMAN
RESOURCES MANAGEMENT

This book favours a practical approach to human resources management; however, good practices should be built on sound theory. It is important to understand key legal concepts that impact on human resources management.

In my experience, even without a good knowledge of the law, you probably will find that you are managing your human resources in a lawful manner so long as you engage in common sense management. Both common sense and the law require that your human resources decisions be exercised in good faith, and with the kind of respect and concern for your people that you would expect in an advanced democracy like Canada.

In this section, we will review the central concept of management rights. We will then examine the boundaries that restrict management in its operation of the workplace. In particular, we will review the boundaries created by centuries of common law, made by judges, and decades of statutory law, made by elected politicians and their legislative assemblies.

In addition to the strict legal boundaries within which employers must operate, there are certain other boundaries that impact on how people are managed in Canadian workplaces. To a very real degree, these additional boundaries are self-imposed. That is, they represent limitations that management quite properly imposes on itself, especially if it is acting knowledgeably and in a responsible manner.

The fundamental starting place is that management can do whatever it wants in pursuit of the objectives of the workplace, subject to the restrictive boundaries. In other words, management does not have to look for permission to do whatever it wants. Instead, management has to look to see if it is restricted or prevented from doing what it wants. If it is not limited by one or more of the boundaries that we will shortly review, then management is free to act as it sees fit.

To put this in a visual context, imagine that you are constructing a one-room house in an open field. You start with the field, stretching out as far as you can see in every direction. That is management in its original state, free to do whatever it wants — what it thinks is necessary to achieve the business or institutional objectives. As we will soon see, this is not a normal house. The boundaries that we are forced to put up in a couple of cases and that we choose to put up in a couple of other cases are not solid, or at least not throughout. There are wide-open spaces in each of the boundaries that maintain considerable freedom for management. The open field remains, but not in all places and not for all purposes.

There are four walls or four boundaries on management rights. Not only are the walls not solid throughout, but also these boundaries are not entirely fixed. Indeed, all of the boundaries are subject to some adjustment through the intervention of management, even though they all remain to some degree as limitations on management's freedom to act. Here are the boundaries that limit the exercise of management rights.

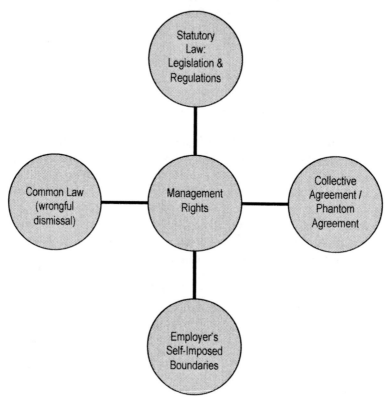

As we proceed to build the four walls of our house, the task of those of you involved in human resources management will be to find ways to achieve what you need to do within the one-room house or to try to modify the limitations created by each boundary. You can only learn to live within the walls or to transform the walls if you achieve an initial understanding of the walls themselves. Please note that, at this point, we will only seek to introduce concepts. Some of the key concepts will be explored more fully further on in these pages.

The First Boundary — The Common Law

The first boundary is the common law. The common law is what is sometimes referred to as judge-made law. In Canada, the common law is derived from our British heritage, and comes to us after almost ten centuries of adjudicating individual disputes. In particular, the common law has taken shape since the invention of the printing press at the end of the 15th century. With increasing ease, the ability to copy text automatically has allowed for the recording and general distribution of decisions. For the most part, the common law that applies to employment relationships is the law of contracts, although there are also elements of the law of torts that can frame a dispute between an employee, the employer and sometimes individual representatives of the employer as well.

The boundary created by the common law is that, if the employer does not treat employees in accordance with the centuries-old expectations of the courts, the employer may find itself at the receiving end of a legal action commenced by an employee, typically following the termination of the employment relationship. Such cases are normally referred to as "wrongful dismissals". Naturally, most employers in most cases would rather avoid the time and money associated with a legal action. For that reason, understanding the common law, and acting in a way that will minimize the possibility that a formal legal proceeding will come into play, effectively creates a self-imposed boundary or restriction on management rights. In other words, in this context, management can do anything that it wants, but it is prudent to act in a manner that is less likely to motivate a dismissed employee to commence or pursue a legal action.

There are three significant components of the common law as it applies to a non-union workplace. The first is that each employee is employed under a contract of employment. The second and third components arise out of the expectation that employers should act as good corporate citizens: management should be reasonably fair and frank in its representation of the key facts of employment, both at the outset of an employment relationship and whenever significant changes are made; furthermore, management should treat employees with reasonable dignity and respect at the time that the employment relationship is terminated, especially if it is terminated by a unilateral decision of management. In the last five years, this third component has led to a particular kind of claim, called *Wallace* damages, named after the 1997 decision of the Supreme Court of Canada that gave birth to the concept: *Wallace v. United Grain Growers Limited*, [1997] 3 S.C.R. 701.

The Law of Contracts

The first and fundamental component of the common law that applies to a non-union workplace comes from the law of contracts. A contract is typically between two parties. It deals with an exchange, where each party gives to the other party something of value. The contract is formed by a bargain that is initiated by the offer of one party and concluded by the acceptance of the other, so long as each side considers that it has benefited from whatever is exchanged between the parties. There are often significant terms and conditions to ensure that the aspects of the exchange retain value for each party for the duration of the contract.

Every employment relationship that exists in Canada between an individual and an employer, from the part-time clerk at the corner grocer to the president of the largest bank, is a contract. In the bargain that is struck between an employee and his or her employer, the individual person is trading physical and mental attributes (brawn and brains), in varying degrees, in return for the compensation package that comes with a job, as well as some degree of security in employment.

Many people think of a contract as a formal legal document, complete with red seals and signed by quill pens. It does not have to be like that. It does not have to be written or it could be that only part of the contract is in writing. It could be made up of different parts, with one part (such as a letter of hire) specifically addressed to the individual employee, and other parts (such as a benefits booklet and employee rules) generally addressed to all employees. Whatever is written to the individual employee could be on the back of a napkin, a letter of hire or something more formal.

The most contentious part of an employment contract has to do with termination of employment. The usual contract of employment in Canada is one of indefinite hire. Unless there is a clear contractual provision, which almost certainly has to be in writing, it will be assumed that an employment relationship has no defined end. Indeed, if there is nothing in writing about termination of employment, and if nothing like that was ever discussed with the employee before hire, then a court would be prepared to imply that the duration of the contract is indefinite.

From what is written above, it will be apparent that it is possible to have a contract for a defined term or task. A defined term means that the employment is for an actual time period and might include a renewal provision. A defined task means that the employment is intended to continue for the duration of a particular event, like the installation of a piece of equipment or the implementation of a computer system, or the opening or closing of a plant. In most cases, written contracts for a defined term or task do not cause legal problems at the end of the contract (the termination of employment) unless the contracts are poorly drafted.

With a contract of indefinite hire, employment will terminate in one of the following ways:

- for cause, in which case the employer typically argues that the employee has engaged in misconduct that is so serious that it constitutes a fundamental breach; typically, this suggests behaviour that is grossly dishonest or disruptive, sometimes to the point of being violent and even criminal; it can also refer to poor performance, especially if that has been documented and the employee has had a chance to improve;
- due to frustration of contract, including death or serious illness or injury, in which case the employee is no longer capable of meeting its side of the employment bargain, to provide physical and mental attributes to the employer on a reasonably regular basis;
- due to business failure, in which case the employees may retain claims in respect of a business that is bankrupt or in receivership, as well as potential claims against directors or other participants in the failed business;

17

- due to a fundamental change in the employee's duties or in other terms and conditions of employment, including but not limited to compensation — this is typically referred to as constructive dismissal;
- due to the employee's own resignation or retirement;
- in accordance with a retirement policy that is actively enforced, even if the employee would prefer not to retire; or
- as a result of providing reasonable notice or pay in lieu of some or all of that notice.

Legal issues may arise in any case of termination of employment. The most common legal claims have to do with the calculation of reasonable notice. In most cases, this really means a dispute about how much the employer has to pay in lieu of reasonable notice. Other common legal arguments arise when an employer claims cause for immediate termination of employment without compensation, or when an employee claims that s/he has been constructively dismissed.

It is important to understand that in most Canadian jurisdictions, subject to certain statutory claims, an employer is within its rights to terminate the employment of a non-union employee. When we talk of wrongful dismissal claims, it is not the dismissal itself that is wrongful. Rather, the wrong that is at the base of such a claim is that the employer did not give enough notice (or pay in lieu of notice), or, in cases of cause, frustration or constructive dismissal, that the employer did not give any notice.

It should be noted as well that an employee could not make a common law claim and then simply sit back and wait for the money to roll in. The law expects that an employee, once terminated from active employment, will make every reasonable effort to find new employment. This is described as the obligation to mitigate damages. If an employee finds other employment, or if the employee fails to make reasonable efforts, then the employer involved in the termination of employment is entitled to an offset to the extent that the mitigation overlaps with the period of reasonable notice.

At Will Employment – A Foreign Concept: Before we carry on, it may be useful to discuss a commonly misunderstood and misapplied concept — employment "at will". Employment at will means there is a presumption that the employee is employed at the employer's will for an indefinite period rather than for a fixed term. Either the employee or employer can end the employment relationship at any time for any reason.

In most American states, unless the parties have entered into a formal agreement orally or in writing, specifying the terms of the employment relationship, employment is deemed to be "at will". For example, Michigan and New York are both "at-will" states.

"At will" employees do have some legal protection. They cannot be fired in violation of federal or state laws, such as prohibitions against discrimination and harassment, and protection for whistleblowers. There may be other public policy reasons to assist employees in the face of oppressive conduct by the employer, or conduct that constitutes a reprisal against the employee in response to the exercise of a statutory right. As well, even where there is no formal employment contract, a court may imply that some statement or document from the employer had the effect of creating an employment contract. Most frequently the basis of an implied contract is an employee handbook or benefits manual distributed by the employer.

HRP's of companies that have American parents or that are otherwise related to or associated with American companies may well come up against the "at will" concept. In particular, they may have to deal with policies or handbooks originating in the United States that include disclaimers intended to reinforce the "at will" nature of employment and thereby defeat the possibility of an implied contract. If you are in such a situation, it is absolutely essential to understand that there is no "at will" concept in Canada. The only way that you can create an equivalent to such a concept is through a very clear written contract of employment. Even then, you will have to ensure that you satisfy minimum employment standards, failing which the contract would not be valid. This may take some explaining if you are an HRP who reports to a senior executive employee who is based in the United States.

The Law of Torts

The second component of the common law that applies to a non-union workplace comes from the law of torts. The law of torts has to do with how people treat each other. Unlike a contract, where two parties make an agreement to deal with each other in a certain way, the law of torts deals with common expectations and understandings that do not need to be part of specific agreements between people. In a civilized society, we expect that people will act in good faith, without violence, and with a proper respect for the property of other people. If these expectations are not met, individual offenders can be criminally prosecuted. They can also be the subject of a separate civil lawsuit.

In the United States, an example of the two different proceedings, criminal and civil, can be found in the notorious O.J. Simpson case. Mr. Simpson, a professional football player, was acquitted of criminal charges related to the death of his wife Nicole and a man named Ronald Goldman. The family of Mr. Goldman subsequently commenced a civil lawsuit that was successful, in which they claimed that Mr. Simpson had wrongfully caused the death of Mr. Goldman and should be liable to the family in damages for all of the losses that would be suffered because Mr. Goldman was no longer alive.

A tort is sometimes, but not necessarily, related to a crime. Many torts involve misconduct that could not be the subject of a criminal prosecution, but which is still widely expected to be subject to sanctions if other people are harmed as a direct and foreseeable consequence of the poor behaviour. In employment situations, employees could commence a legal action against the employer and, as we will see, sometimes other employees as well.

The law of torts has not been particularly significant in the employment context to date, but there have been some high profile and noteworthy court decisions, especially in the past twenty years. As a result, claims arising from the manner in which an employee has been treated, as opposed to the law of the employment contract, may become much more prominent in the future. At root, these cases are based in the concept of reasonable and frank representation of key facts of employment. The court expects truth, or at least the avoidance of deceit, and a certain degree of diligence when it comes to making representations about a job. It is not enough for employer representatives to be honest, they must also be reasonably well informed, so that they do not "honestly" misrepresent key facts because of a lack of knowledge.

Just as a house built on sand is doomed to fall, an employment relationship is fundamentally flawed if it is based on deceit, misstatements, misleading information or recklessness on the part of the employer or its representatives. Indeed, even if there is a written contract of employment in such a situation, it may be voided by the court, entitling the employee to significant remedies under both tort law and contract law without regard to the written document.

20

If a representative of the employer holds out that s/he has the authority to enter into an employment contract on behalf of the employer, then a special relationship is created with the job applicant in the context of the hiring process. This is also true for existing employees in situations of promotion or re-assignment. Representatives who are decision makers or who act in that manner have to expect that the targets of their representations will act on the basis of the statements made (and perhaps the information concealed) by the representatives. There is a special duty of care to be respected by these employer representatives. In enforcing this special duty, the court takes account of the fact that there is relatively little cost in ensuring that managers who hire or promote are given carefully prepared and correct information. By contrast, it would be extremely costly, if not impossible in many instances, for employees or prospective hires to verify the accuracy of the representations made by these managers.

A careful representative must not represent material facts to the employee or prospective hire that the representative knows, or ought to know, are wrong or misleading. No person can be expected to know the future; however, if the present reality of a company is materially different from what is represented to an employee or prospective hire, then it may be the foundation for a claim for damages. For example, if an applicant for a position at a plant in Toronto inquires about whether or not the plant is likely to remain stable or in a growth mode, then it could be a negligent misrepresentation to provide such reassurance when there are in fact active plans to close the plant.

The law has little interest in cases where no real harm is done. To have a valid claim, the applicant in our Toronto plant example must act on the basis of the representation. The applicant must rely on the representation to his or her detriment. The reliance must be reasonable. A clear example of reasonable and detrimental reliance would be if the applicant were to leave secure and long-term employment only to find out six months later that the plant is closing. On the other hand, it likely would not be reasonable for an applicant to rely on information that the applicant knows to be untrue or at least questionable.

Law is dynamic. As this area of the law evolves, it may be that there will be not only a prohibition against deceit and negligent misstatement, but also a requirement to make representations about relevant facts that are within the knowledge of the employer, but would not be obvious to a prospective employee. Using the same example of the doomed Toronto plant, it may be that a job applicant has to be told about the likely future of the plant even if there is no such inquiry initiated by the applicant. Indeed, it may be that representatives of an employer who have recruitment and hiring responsibilities have to engage in ongoing due diligence about their own companies, to ensure that current information about the employer that is relevant is communicated to a job applicant in a timely and proactive manner. Naturally, any such legal principle will depend on such particular facts as the position and the legitimate expectations of the prospective employee, as well as the degree of certainty of the information in question. You can imagine how tricky this could become if the decision about the plant is not final, or is not general knowledge. The court is often required to strike a balance. In this case, the balance would be between the interest of the employee or the prospective hire in being able to make rational career decisions, and the employer's interest in protecting its confidential information and in keeping the costs of preparing such information within reasonable bounds.

In any event, and subject to the peculiarities that exist with any unique set of facts, the general rule for employers should be that their representatives should conduct themselves in a manner that is always honest and reasonably frank and complete. This should be so in meetings with employees and prospective employees, and also in terms of the disclosure of material facts and information in situations of hire or promotion. Dishonesty and evasion could lead to exposure, not only for the employer, but also, on an individual basis, for the representative who is the cause of the problem. This could be particularly important in the event that a company has financial problems, as the dishonest or negligent representative could remain directly liable for damages as an individual defendant.

The consequences of reckless or dishonest behaviour on behalf of representatives of the employer could be dire. There could be damages for lost income and job search expenses while the employee finds other employment, as well as losses suffered from relocation if the employee moved in order to take the job in the first place or has to move to find new employment. There also could be damages for emotional distress. As far as existing employees are concerned, there could be damages for lost opportunities if an employee chooses to continue employment as a result of statements made by a representative of the employer that are reckless or known by the representative to be untrue. Contractual concepts like probationary periods or specified notice periods or severance payments are irrelevant to these kinds of claims, whether by new hires or existing employees, and would have no limiting effect on the damages that could be claimed.

It is possible to create contractually a disclaimer that takes away the employer's responsibility for the truth of any representations made and puts the burden entirely on the new hire to be satisfied about the soundness of the employment relationship. At the very least, this disclaimer must be clearly and comprehensively drafted, and it should be brought to the new hire's attention before or simultaneously with making the representations, and certainly before employment is actually commenced. Having raised the possibility of such a disclaimer, I must comment that it is a poor start to an employment relationship to tell an employee that s/he should not rely on the representations that are being made by the manager responsible for recruitment and hiring. A court will have little sympathy for the employer in such a situation and would delight in finding flaws in the drafting or hiring process, such that a contractual disclaimer would not invalidate a claim in tort.

It is important for employer representatives not to be unduly fearful as a result of this discussion of the consequences of deceit or negligent misstatements. These are not trivial matters and claims cannot be founded on a base of normal communications. Employer representatives are entitled to be optimistic and opinionated about the employer. Expectations of future growth and prosperity are not deceitful and do not constitute negligent misstatements just because the anticipated or hoped for growth does not materialize, unless the expectations arise from assumptions that have no reasonable basis in fact. The concern is with present-day facts, which have to be honestly represented and reasonably factored into assumptions and future forecasts. The courts have no concern with rosy futures that do not come to pass as a result of future events that could not have been foreseen. Representatives can still be enthusiastic salespersons. The courts do not expect representatives to be prophets or to have reliable crystal balls.

Wallace Damages

The third component is a gloss that has been added to the common law of contracts. As a result of the *Wallace* decision (cited on page 16), the conduct of an employer at the point of dismissal may affect a court's assessment of the damages owing to the employee.

As discussed above, in the absence of just cause and in the absence of an express contractual provision dealing with termination of employment, an employee is generally entitled to receive reasonable notice of dismissal. Absent such notice, there is typically entitlement to damages in lieu of reasonable notice to compensate for the breach.

In the last twenty years, the courts have been encouraged by lawyers for employees to loosen the stranglehold of the traditional contractual notion of reasonable notice. Plaintiffs have sought aggravated damages for mental distress caused by the dismissal. Defendant employers have presented a variety of obstacles to such claims, including causation, remoteness, medical proof of mental distress and limitations in the courts' ability to make reasonable inferences as to the intention of the parties in framing the contract. As a result, there were increasingly artificial legal arguments built more on hyperbole than on facts or a logical legal analysis.

With *Wallace*, the Supreme Court of Canada tried to cut through the nonsense while at the same time holding employers accountable for the dismissal process. The Court made it clear that aggravated damages may be awarded to a plaintiff only where the acts of the employer or its representatives that gave rise to the injury were independently actionable. The failure to give reasonable notice is not, itself, likely to be sufficient to cause mental distress. Courts must be shown something more, such as a verbal or physical assault or a fraudulent misrepresentation.

Having made it more difficult for a plaintiff to claim aggravated damages, the Supreme Court of Canada in *Wallace* then provided plaintiffs with a way around the issue. The employer is probably not required as a matter of contract to act fairly and in good faith in making dismissal decisions, and the act of dismissal by itself does not likely create a tort. That said, and probably as a matter of public policy more than legal theory, the Court determined that the period of reasonable notice could be extended in situations where the employer demonstrates bad faith or dismisses an employee in an unfair manner that causes mental suffering for the employee. In other words, if the employee can provide compelling evidence of mental suffering on the one hand and bad conduct by the employer on the other, the employee does not have to worry about the legal obstacles that employers have relied on in defence of claims for aggravated damages.

Although it has cleared up much of the mess caused by the push for aggravated damages, *Wallace* has introduced a new element of uncertainty and potential for judicial creativity that has not been welcome news for employers. Absent a clear contractual provision, calculating damages in lieu of reasonable notice always has been more art than science. Now it is more so. Plaintiffs now routinely claim *Wallace* damages on even the flimsiest facts, which creates one more bargaining chip and one more obstacle in the settlement process.

Although the law is not entirely settled in this respect, it is at least arguable that *Wallace* has no application in cases where the notice period is contractually specified. That is, when the employer has entered into a pre-employment or (less clearly) a pre-promotion contract with a new hire or employee that sets out the notice period or payments to be made in the event of dismissal, then the court should have no role to play in determining the reasonable period of notice. As such, the use of well defined notice periods in written employment contracts should become increasingly popular with employers wishing to prevent the courts from using *Wallace* to increase the period of reasonable notice. Unfortunately for employers, given what I consider to be a rather uncertain legal basis for the policy-driven *Wallace* doctrine, I expect that the courts will remain open to invitations to apply *Wallace* even in the face of a clearly drafted written contract.

The Second Boundary — Statutory Law

Even after centuries of evolution, judge-made law had at least a couple of major drawbacks. First, a court could only deal with the particular set of facts that would come before it in each case. This kind of scattershot evolution led to holes in the law, as well as inconsistencies between cases. Second, as there was no real plan or rule book, the common law did not naturally take a leadership role in building a just society.

Statutory law is the law that is made by elected politicians. Statutory law began to have a significant impact on workplaces in the latter part of the nineteenth century, after the first few generations of industrial revolution in Europe, and with the rapid evolution of the new democracies in North America. Most of the important statutory law that affects our workplaces has been developed since World War II.

In Canada, employment law in its statutory form is made primarily by provincial legislatures. The federal government has fairly narrow jurisdiction that covers federal institutions and organizations like banks, telecommunication companies, cable companies, and companies involved in inter-provincial transportation (not an exhaustive list). Provincial governments are responsible for almost all manufacturing activity, mining, construction and most of the service industries.

Statutory law is a significant tool that governments can use in order to put their political agendas into effect. By its nature, statutory law allows political parties elected to power to change fundamental rules that govern society. Statutory law can fill in the holes left by the common law and smooth out real and perceived inequities or inconsistencies.

The five most significant areas of statutory law in the workplace are:

- **Employment standards** — these standards set the floor for workplaces in Canada, such that you have to meet at least the minimum statutory requirements in order to operate a business; most businesses exceed the minimum standards to a significant degree.

- **Labour law**, or the law of trade unions — this is the law that determines how a trade union gets certified to act as the sole and exclusive agent for a group of employees, what obligations are thereby created for the employer of those employees, and what is the framework to govern the relationship between the union and the employer in respect of the affected group of employees.

- **Health and safety** — there is an internal responsibility system in Canada that places the obligation on the various workplace players to co-exist and co-operate in safe and healthy workplace environments; this is achieved in large part by providing worker representatives and health and safety committees with significant powers to become informed and to bring unsafe or unhealthy conditions to the attention of the employer.

- **Workers' compensation** or workplace safety and insurance — this is the insurance system run by the various provincial governments that provides a complex system of benefits to workers who are injured or who become ill because of workplace situations, in return for which workers give up the right to sue their employers for creating the unsafe or unhealthy situation or for allowing it to continue.
- **Human rights**, including laws dealing with equity in pay and employment — this is the relatively recent area of workplace law that has become a fundamental force in the western world following World War II; essentially this area of the law mandates that people must be hired and promoted in the workplace without regard to such external characteristics as race, culture, gender, age, or even handicap.

Statutory law also created powerful administrative tribunals, bureaucracies and civil servants, including labour relations boards, human rights commissions, health and safety inspectors, employment standards officers and workers' compensation boards.

Let us take a closer look at how each of the above areas of statutory law creates restrictions on the rights of management to do whatever it wants in operating the workplace. The intention is not to provide a mini-review of each area of legislative intervention. Rather, the main objective is to gain an understanding of the nature of the restrictions on management rights in each area.

Employment Standards

The floor plan created by employment standards legislation covers the fundamental terms and conditions of any employment relationship, although often at a very basic level. On the compensation side, a minimum wage is established, but there is little or no guidance provided in respect of benefits or pension plans. Statutory holiday and vacation entitlements are set out. There are detailed pregnancy leave rights, and other unpaid leaves may be described. Significant obligations are created for situations of termination of employment or lengthy lay-offs. There are also important obligations established for employers to maintain records. The employment standards bureaucracy is given the usual powers of investigation, and each statute has a mechanism for the adjudication of disputes.

Employment standards legislation should be used at the front end and the back end of any framework for human resources management. At the front end, the basic elements of employment standards legislation are a good starting point for the framework. At the back end, it is important to check the framework against employment standards requirements to ensure that nothing has been missed and nothing is offside.

Labour Law, the Law of Trade Unions

There are two key parts to the statutory law dealing with trade unions. The first part describes how a trade union acquires the legal right to represent employees in a workplace — this is the process of certification. The second part sets out a trade union's rights and an employer's obligations once the trade union is certified — the most important of these deals with the negotiation of the collective agreement. The collective agreement is a written deal between the employer and union that covers the terms and conditions of employment, which thereby forms the contractual framework within which the employer, the employees, and the union representatives must operate. The collective agreement is, in effect, the private legislation of the workplace, designed to limit the exercise of management rights.

Through direct negotiations, the parties establish the provisions of the collective agreement. However, if the parties are unable to reach agreement through direct negotiations, they have recourse to a lawful strike/lockout in accordance with labour relations legislation. A lawful work stoppage will continue until such time as the parties resume negotiations to resolve any outstanding issues and thereby establish a new collective agreement.

Naturally, non-union employers should be most concerned about the first part, which is how unions get organized, in the hope that they never get to the second part, which focuses on the creation of the collective agreement. That said, there are elements in the second part beyond the collective bargaining itself that are useful to consider in terms of what a collective agreement is and what some of its key components are.

As to the first part, which deals with a union's bargaining rights, the starting point is the notion of a bargaining unit and a trade union representative of the unit. For the most part, the bargaining unit

28

consists of a grouping of workers of a single employer, either at a single location or within a geographical area that is typically the size of a municipality, county, or something similar. It is typical to group blue-collar workers separately from white-collar workers. As well, there are certain trades or professions, like operating engineers, nurses and security guards, which have their own distinct units, either by law or by historical convention. Management employees are excluded from bargaining units, as are workers with confidential functions related to labour relations; however, the dividing line can vary from jurisdiction to jurisdiction and even from case to case.

From the above, if you are a non-union employer, you have to understand that any of your workers in a plant or office could be subject to union organizing activity. The union organizing may target different groupings of workers, but it is essentially a blue collar/white collar split, with management employees excluded. For this reason alone, you should be clear about the status of your supervisors and the distinction between a supervisor and a worker who has responsibilities as a group leader or lead hand. You also should be clear about those workers who have positions that involve significant elements of confidentiality. If you have multiple plants or offices within a municipality-like geographical area, then you have to be aware that you could end up with a grouping of employees that extends to your multiple locations, although you remain vulnerable as well at each individual location.

If you are concerned that labour law makes it easy for trade unions to organize, your concern is exactly the point. It is supposed to be easy. So long as a trade union has the majority support of a group of workers that is viable for purposes of collective bargaining, the law takes the view that a unionized workplace is preferable and that workers should be entitled to union representation.

All jurisdictions in Canada allow for organizing drives, in which trade unions attempt to have employees sign union membership cards. Membership at this stage costs little or nothing. In some jurisdictions, all that a union has to do is to sign up enough employees in the bargaining unit and that will suffice for the certificate. In other jurisdictions, notably Ontario, signing cards is a necessary precondition to a representation vote, but the union requires the support of the majority of those who vote in a secret-ballot election before a certificate will be granted.

In all jurisdictions, an employer must conduct itself during an organizing drive with reasonable restraint. Neither threats to job security nor promises of better compensation in return for the union's defeat are acceptable. A union can raise allegations of misconduct at the Labour Relations Board, which has wide remedial powers, which vary from jurisdiction to jurisdiction. Free speech is still the hallmark of our democracy, so an employer retains significant rights of expression during the organizing campaign. It is generally important at this stage to retain legal counsel to help you design a campaign of appropriate response to an organizing drive and to make judgment calls about the legality of specific actions. Law is rarely black or white; it comes in many shades of grey. That is particularly true when it comes to making determinations about the limits to be respected by an employer in the face of an aggressive organizing drive.

If a union is successful in achieving a certificate, it is thereafter recognized as the sole and exclusive bargaining agent for a defined group of employees. Although there are processes to terminate the bargaining rights of a union, it is very difficult to get rid of a union once it has been certified. As a result, unions represent workers who actively campaigned against them, as well as new workers who were never involved in the organizing campaign and who never made an individual choice about whether or not they want a union. Indeed, in time, a workplace will become full of workers who did not actually choose the union. Most of these will be relatively apathetic about the ongoing role of the union. Some will become active supporters and others will remain hostile, either to this particular union or to unions in general.

With a certified trade union in place, we turn briefly to the second part of labour legislation. In all jurisdictions, the employer must bargain in good faith with a view to achieving a collective agreement. If collective bargaining breaks down, then a legal strike or lockout will, in most cases, follow a government supervised conciliation process. Most such work stoppages eventually end in a settlement, although often not until several weeks have passed. Some work stoppages lead to a complete breakdown in the relationship, which may result in a shutdown of the operation and an ongoing stalemate. In some situations and some sectors a breakdown in collective bargaining will lead to "interest" arbitration, in which a neutral adjudicator will determine the outstanding issues and thereby settle the collective agreement.

Almost all collective agreements share these common characteristics, whether settled through consensual bargaining, conciliation, mediation, impasse bargaining during a work stoppage, or arbitration, and whether required by law or expected by convention:

1. recognition of the union as the bargaining agent for a defined group of employees;

2. recognition of management rights, except as restricted by the collective agreement or law;

3. automatic deduction of union dues;

4. recognition of union representatives;

5. prohibition against work stoppages during the term of the collective agreement;

6. a term of at least one year and typically two or three years, sometimes longer; note that by the time some collective agreements are settled, the term is already partially or even completely over and it is time to start negotiations all over again;

7. seniority provisions, including clauses dealing with promotions and lay-offs;

8. provisions dealing with hours of work, overtime, and premium time, such as weekends and night shifts;

9. vacation, holiday and leave provisions;

10. compensation, including classifications, wages, perquisites, benefits, and sometimes pension plans; and

11. a formal procedure to deal with complaints, called the grievance procedure, including access to arbitration as the final stage for resolution of disputes.

As we will see below, dealing with the "phantom" collective agreement, many of the elements of a collective agreement can be very instructive in a non-union workplace, particularly items 7 through 11. Even some of the items 1 to 6 can have an impact. It is useful to define groups of employees; the concept of management rights should be widely understood; employee representatives, both formal and informal, can play a key role in a non-union workplace; and there should be a regular review of the policies, procedures, practices and rules that are the tools of human resources management, in much the same way as would be required for a collective agreement.

Health and Safety

It is a moral duty, as well as a legal requirement, that employers in Canada co-operate with their employees in order to operate safe and healthy workplaces. It is unfortunate that this is an obligation that is much clearer and more keenly felt after a serious accident. It is important to embrace healthy and safe practices from the earliest possible opportunity. A very useful strategy is to look for "near-misses", where no worker is hurt but there could have been injuries either with bad luck or bad timing. If you can find or create near-misses, then you can use those to teach healthy and safe practices in a very meaningful manner.

For non-union workplaces, health and safety law provides an ideal opportunity to create leadership opportunities for your workers. It is also a natural setting for co-operation between workers and management. Any time you can create and reinforce "us", you make it more difficult for a union to organize, as unions thrive on the existence or creation of an adversarial relationship between workers and management.

As a matter of law, management and workers are required to co-operate in creating and maintaining a healthy and safe workplace. The internal responsibility system, which is the basis for Canadian health and safety law, places the onus on the workplace participants to create a good working environment. The role of government is to resolve disputes and to ensure that the system is functioning as it should; otherwise, the system features self-monitoring, self-improvement and self-regulation for the most part. Workers are entitled to have input through regular inspections and committee meetings. They are entitled to make recommendations through meeting minutes that must be considered by the employer. Workers can properly expect management to respond in an effective and timely fashion to reasonable suggestions for improving the workplace environment.

Sensible employers should embrace this part of the statutory boundary with enthusiasm. Going the extra mile to encourage and facilitate effective meetings, recommendations and employee input will pay off, not only in terms of the important objective of having a healthy and safe workplace, but also in terms of creating a team of workers and management with a common objective.

Sensible employers should also continue to take the lead in matters of health and safety. Although it is a shared responsibility and there is more scope for worker input here than anywhere else, short of unionization, it is ultimately the employer and the members of the management team that will bear responsibility in the event of a serious accident or fatality. As a result, it is important for the employer to keep current a comprehensive safety policy, to implement procedures for safe operation and dealing with accidents or unsafe incidents, to teach safe practices, and to impose rules against unsafe practices with disciplinary consequences. Consistent with the co-operative nature of health and safety, worker input is very helpful in all of these respects and is probably the best way to raise the profile of health and safety in the workplace. Indeed, effective and ongoing opportunities for input in the development of policies, procedures and rules can result in the employees training themselves to a significant extent.

Safety is a hot button issue and, regardless of the best efforts of non-union employers, is likely to be featured in any union organizing campaign. You can never get rid of safety as an issue. You can never erase the memory of a serious accident. The best you can do is to focus on health and safety issues with serious intent, and to demonstrate to your workers that you are prepared to listen to their concerns and ideas, and to take action that is appropriate and reasonable.

Workers' Compensation

Workers' compensation (workplace safety and insurance in Ontario) is really the flip side of health and safety law. To the extent that accidents occur in a workplace, or illnesses develop, there is a decades-old insurance scheme (since as early as 1915 in Ontario) that provides benefits to workers on the one hand and, on the other hand, protects employers from employee lawsuits.

The two key elements of workers' compensation from the standpoint of effective management of human resources are accurate and timely reporting, and aggressive return-to-work initiatives.

Workers need to be able to trust management. They need to know that, if they have a claim, management will view it as a priority to report promptly and completely. Similarly, if management has doubts about an injury or illness, they owe it to all other employees to raise those doubts in a frank and fair manner, with appropriate opportunity for response. Once workers get a sense that their fellow workers are able to play with the system, the integrity of the system will be seriously harmed and other workers may be tempted to abuse it.

If workers are absent from the workplace due to illness or injury, then management should closely track the progress of the worker and aggressively seek out opportunities to return the worker to the workplace as quickly as possible. It is common for a worker to come back to modified work and even modified hours. There may be a work-trial period, typically lasting four to eight weeks, during which the worker can get up to speed, either at his or her former job or at a suitably modified job that is still useful to the employer.

Modified work exacts a price, on the employer, the worker in question and co-workers. The employer is, hopefully, still getting reasonable productivity from the worker, but less than optimal productivity. The worker is unable to work at his or her full potential and may well be suffering some income loss as a result. Co-workers may have to shoulder both inconvenience and heavier or more difficult work. Alternatively, co-workers may lose the opportunity to access job vacancies that involve lighter work and perhaps even higher pay, as preference for those positions may be given to workers with disabilities. As a result, modified work should be viewed as temporary. Every effort should be made to return the worker to full or regular duties as soon as possible. Failure to do so by a non-union employer could have a negative impact on the morale of the work force and could breed dissension, especially if it becomes a pattern and is not isolated to infrequent situations.

If it becomes apparent that permanent modifications are necessary, because the worker has reached a point of maximum medical recovery, then it is important that the employer reorganize the workplace in a permanent way to accommodate the disability. Stop-gap solutions that may be appropriate for a short period of work-trial or for a temporary period while medical recovery is ongoing are rarely appropriate in the longer term. Indeed, in some cases, and subject to a close analysis of human rights and workers' compensation requirements, it may be determined that permanent accommodation is not possible.

Increasingly, workers' compensation is not simply a system for compensating workers who become ill or injured as a result (at least in part) of workplace activities. Workers' compensation has become focused on rehabilitation of injured workers and returning them to active employment, preferably at their former workplaces. An employer has legal obligations to accommodate such workers. An employer can enhance its reputation and stature with the workers by demonstrating compassion and flexibility. At the same time, an employer must not lose sight of the disruptive and negative impact that modified work can have on the workplace if it is not properly and diligently managed. Dissension breeds fastest if there is a sense of injustice between employees, where some think that others are getting away with a lighter load.

Non-union workplaces that do a poor job of balancing the interests of injured workers with the interests of other workers in the plant are vulnerable to union organizers, whichever way the imbalance tilts. Unions, with some justification, can portray themselves as expert advocates for injured workers. At the same time, unions can reassure the other workers that, with a collective agreement, and with union representatives active in such areas as modified work, accommodation, ergonomics and health and safety, the workplace can be made to be a better, more equitable place for all workers.

Human Rights

We have already introduced some human rights issues in dealing with the rehabilitation and return to work of injured workers. Essentially, human rights law for workplace purposes is divided into two parts: discrimination and harassment. The prohibitions against discrimination are based on the notion that an employer should recruit, hire and promote without regard to external characteristics, focusing only on the real skills, abilities and qualifications of each person. The prohibitions against harassment are based on the notion that all persons should be free from abuse from co-workers and supervisors that arises from their external characteristics, gender and race or culture in particular.

Discrimination can arise directly because of the improper conduct and attitudes of decision-makers. It also can be indirect or constructive in nature, insofar as it arises from barriers to effective recruitment, hiring and promotion practices. For example, if an employer recruits through word-of-mouth referrals from existing employees, then you are simply perpetuating the existing social, economic and cultural makeup of the organization. Potentially, you are missing out on significant groups in your community that may have qualified and motivated candidates for employment. If you have tests or physical qualifications that are not reasonably related to the work for which you are hiring, then you may be screening out applicants who are perfectly capable. If you value paper qualifications over work experience in promotion situations, then you may be missing out on skilled workers who have not succeeded in formal schooling or training because of learning disabilities that would not impact on the quality or quantity of their work. Some of these misplaced barriers may be illegal as contrary to human rights legislation; others may be simply bad for business.

Failure to prevent harassment between employees can lead to a poisoned workplace. Unhappily, the workers who tend to leave such an environment are the victims. The employer is left with the bigoted, sexist or simply ignorant creeps who have engaged in the misconduct in the first place. Remember basic management rights: you have the right to create the workplace that you want. By law, you have the obligation to prevent harassment. Racial humour, sexual banter and innuendo, graphic posters, and crude language are not welcome in your workplace if you say so. You set the standard. Here, the standard should be set high and there should be little tolerance for contravention of the standard. That is what the law expects of management. You have the right, and probably the obligation, to insist on a civil workplace.

Puritanical zeal is not required. Nobody expects or even wants your workplace to be cleansed of shop talk, friendly banter, and normal human interaction. There is a line, however, and for the most part, it is a pretty bright line. In most cases, crossing the line is obvious and should not be tolerated. Victims of misconduct deserve to be protected. Those who are unwilling to respect the dignity and self-worth of co-workers should be disciplined and, if necessary, dismissed.

Naturally, you will have little hope of enforcing standards that discourage harassment if your supervisors and managerial staff are not prepared to provide leadership in this area. The law recognizes two particular forms of managerial misconduct in relation to sex: solicitation and reprisal. These are really two sides of the same coin. In each case, a person who is in a position to confer or deny a benefit uses his (it is for the most part not "her") influence in an effort to gain a sexual advantage. Solicitation involves a promise of a benefit, such as a raise, time off or a promotion, in return for a sexual favour. Reprisal involves the threat of loss if a sexual favour is not granted or as pay-back for being spurned. The most obvious loss would be the job itself, but there are many less obvious consequences that an authority figure could visit upon a subordinate worker that could be devastating in their cumulative effect. An employer should have little or no tolerance for supervisors who engage in solicitation or reprisal activities.

For the most part, engaging in effective human rights practices is good for the proper conduct of business in your organization and it should make the group stronger. Non-union workplaces that are not prepared to take a clear and leading role in respect of human rights issues simply leave themselves exposed to union campaigners. After all, if the employer were not prepared to protect its vulnerable workers, a union would be only too happy to volunteer its services.

The Third Boundary — The Phantom Collective Agreement

With statutory law, trade unions acquired the right to represent a group of employees and to compel the employer to bargain a collective agreement that would set out the fundamental terms and conditions of employment. Further, such other statutory laws as employment standards, occupational health and safety, workers' compensation and human rights create the framework for the terms and conditions that appear in the collective agreement.

Non-union workplaces are, in many respects, more difficult to manage from a human resources standpoint. Without the structure of the collective agreement, which also incorporates and organizes many of the statutory requirements, non-union workplaces can be, quite literally, not organized. To help non-union workplaces organize themselves, without a union doing it for them, my recommendation is to create a phantom collective agreement.

Implementing The Concept: A Single Document or A Multi-Layered Framework

Whether they know it or not, and with more or less planning and systematic thinking, non-union workplaces end up implementing many of the terms and conditions that are in a collective agreement. A major recommendation of this book, to which we will return in chapter 4 and afterwards, is that non-union workplaces should become much more informed about typical terms and conditions that apply in unionized workplaces.

Once they become informed, non-union workplaces should be much more deliberate in introducing as many of those terms and conditions as may be appropriate, in a form that is suitable for each individual workplace. This kind of thought-out structure for non-union workplaces, that begs, borrows, or outright steals from comparable union workplaces, is what I consider to be the creation of the phantom collective agreement. The phantom collective agreement either will help to prevent union organizing, or it will help to defend against it if it occurs.

If you adopt this concept of a phantom collective agreement, some non-union workplaces may want to gather terms and conditions of employment, as well as certain aspects of policies and procedures, into a single document or binder that runs parallel to what might be found in a collective agreement. I expect that most non-union workplaces will not want to be so literal. Instead, they will attempt to deal with each of the key issues that appear in a collective agreement at different places within a multi-layered framework for human resources management. I predict that you will have good success with either approach.

Replicating Terms and Conditions of Collective Agreements

Collective agreements contain a significant number and variety of provisions that do not contradict an efficient and effective non-union operation. If you can provide for the same rights, benefits or opportunities, then a union will have fewer arguments to seduce your members if and when an organizing drive comes to your plant or operation. In acting this way, you should also end up with a much better and more efficiently managed workplace.

As set out above, there are some obvious parts of collective agreements that should be considered in a non-union workplace, in particular items 7 through 11, dealing with seniority, work schedules, absences from the workplace, all aspects of compensation, and a complaints procedure. The following additional and supplementary points should be considered in the creation of a phantom agreement:

- there should be a clear description of the major employee groupings — in other words, who are the workplace players;
- you will have to consider ways in which the employees can appoint representatives and situations in which such representatives would have a role to play in the workplace;
- seniority will have much less relevance to a non-union workplace, although an employee's long service always merits some degree of recognition;
- you may want to consider commitments to ongoing training and dealing with workplace changes brought about by new technology or new processes; and
- you should be able to come up with an efficient and multi-layered complaint procedure, although you may have considerable difficulty replacing the arbitration procedure that is required in all unionized workplaces.

Two themes bear repeating. Most of these concepts are necessary for a non-union workplace in any event, such that the phantom collective agreement provides an opportunity for organization and communication of important aspects of human resources management. Secondly, to the extent that an employer can provide the kinds of concepts that would certainly result from collective bargaining, the employer is cutting into the union's sales pitch. Why should an employee pay union dues when s/he is already the recipient of the benefits of unionization?

The Fourth Boundary — Self-Imposed Boundaries

For our purposes, the self-imposed boundaries are not obvious ones, such as capital budgets, cash flow, and the overall purpose of the production or services in which the organization is engaged. Rather, we are talking about key employment concepts such as policies, procedures, practices, rules, culture and history of the workplace. Let us take a closer look at how these are distinctive and yet work together as a cohesive whole.

Policies

Policies are those wide-reaching concepts of human resources management that are fundamental to the effective management of the work force. These are usually carefully considered, regularly reviewed, and written down in a formal manner. Some policies are either required by law or at least widely expected to be in place, such as safety, dealing with harassment, and avoiding discriminatory practices in situations of hiring and promotion. Other policies may include such issues as attendance management, discipline, job evaluation, seniority and training.

Procedures

Procedures are more mechanical than policies and involve the practical steps required to get things done, including implementation of the policies themselves. Procedures usually fall into two general categories. First, there are the procedures that are important to the employer in terms of producing the goods or providing the services that are fundamental to the objectives of the organization. Second, there are the procedures that are important to employees in terms of getting the entitlements, benefits and perquisites that compensate the employees for the work they perform and that allow the employees to integrate work reasonably into the other aspects of their lives.

Some important procedures include all manner of operational issues, as well as employee complaints, calling in absences, performance evaluation, filling job vacancies, applying for leaves, and vacation scheduling. Procedures should be written out in some descriptive fashion. Procedures are often accompanied by notices posted on bulletin boards or in other areas of the workplace, as well as forms generated or controlled by HRP's.

There are at least three important observations about procedures that would improve the operation of any workplace in terms of human resources management:

- Procedures often constitute the detailed and concrete action plan for human resources policies. As such, from a practical standpoint, they are often incorporated into policies or appended to policies. From another direction, procedures can also be the specific articulation of long-standing practices, whether those practices relate to operational issues or aspects of human resources management. Understanding procedures in these contexts should assist in terms of overall consistency and design.

- Procedures are meant to be read, not simply by HRP's and management. Procedures are meant to be read by workers and other categories of employees. The beneficiaries or targets of the procedures have to read them. There should not be binders of procedures carefully locked away in the HRP's cabinets. Instead, there should be booklets distributed and posted that are easy to absorb. Revisions should be made on a periodic basis and updates should be re-distributed from time to time. If you have a booklet of policies and procedures, distribute it, make sure that your workers understand it is important, and re-distribute it every two or three years. Bear in mind that this is essentially what unionized organizations have to do with their collective agreements.

- Many of your workers may not have graduated from high school, let alone benefitted from post-secondary education. For many, English will not be their first language. Everyone, even university graduates, can better absorb short words, short sentences, short paragraphs and focused points. Use pictures, charts and diagrams. Use videos and photographs. Use internal websites and PowerPoint presentations. Remember always that you are not trying to write a university paper, you are trying to communicate something that is important to the operation of your organization. Use all of the communication tools available to you. Whatever you do and however you do it, keep it straightforward and simple ("KISS").

Practices

Practices are often unwritten and largely unnoticed because they are so obvious and widespread. They are the daily, weekly and monthly routines that are straightforward and repetitive and that are predominant in the workplace. Practices deal with such everyday expectations as when employees are expected to be at their workstations, when breaks are taken, how new work is assigned, how overtime is assigned, how absent employees are replaced, and how to deal with machine breakdowns and excessive scrap or unnecessary delays in providing services.

Rules

Rules are specific and narrow. Whereas policies deal in a wide manner with big issues, rules deal with simple issues that can be understood quickly, with obvious consequences for non-compliance. You must wear safety equipment. You may not wear safety shoes or uniforms except at the workplace or for work purposes. You must follow the procedures for safe operation of equipment. You must not engage in horseplay. You must attend work on time. You must not leave your workstation without permission from your supervisor. You must not smoke except in designated areas. These are examples of direct rules that identify proper conduct. Breaching the rules and engaging in misconduct should lead to disciplinary action. Serious or repetitive breaches should lead to dismissal, likely for cause.

The golden rule for rules is that you should be able to put them on one page – two pages if you use pictures, diagrams and charts. If Moses was able to display the Ten Commandments on two stone tablets, you should be able to get workplace rules onto a page or two. To pick on a mistake that I have seen in many organizations, do not try to cram thirty disciplinary rules into a four-page foldout. Eyes will glaze over before your workers make it to the second page. Not even your supervisors will know anything after rule ten. If you need that many disciplinary rules, break them up into categories and post them separately. As with the third observation made above about procedures, "KISS". Use short words and short sentences. Use bullet points to replace paragraphs. Focus on the specific point that is the foundation for your rule.

Rules are not meant to trick your workers or to catch them on fine points. Rules are meant to be followed. You want your workers to know about all of your rules and to understand them. It is therefore essential to communicate your rules so that they will be easily understood.

Culture and History

Workplaces can develop their own personalities. In modern society, each of us spends an incredible amount of time working and in the company of our work-mates. Nobody just punches in and out. Everybody does some living at work, although some are much more connected to workplace events and situations than is the case for others. Workplaces breed friendships, enemies and even intimate relationships, both inside and outside marriage. Many workers socialize with each other, while others avoid their co-workers outside the workplace and sometimes inside as well.

In many workplaces, human resources managers and senior management typically have a much faster turnover rate than is the case for workers and front-line supervisors. In our fast-moving economy, it is normal to find private sector workplaces in which the workers have survived a number of ownership changes and even more changes in leadership. For new management, it is absolutely imperative that you find out about the history of the workplace and that you get a sense of its personality or its culture before you try to stamp on a new identity.

Change is inevitable and often very beneficial, but the pace of change has to be thought out carefully. Rapid and abrupt change can be very disorienting for employees and damaging to a workplace, even if the ultimate direction of the change is positive. On the other hand, slow and deliberate change may be entirely inappropriate in a crisis situation, where shock treatment is probably much more in order.

The worst of all worlds, which happens more often than is sensible, is when the direction of a workplace swings back and forth with each leadership change, without any real regard for what has gone on over the long run and not simply in the latest incarnation of management. In those cases, there will be a kind of underground leadership that develops, where employees tune out management directives and revert to an unwritten way of doing things. Front line supervisors may become similarly disillusioned. As a result, they may consciously, or through inactivity, work in league with the rebellious workers without much regard for the policies, procedures and rules that new management is trying to impose on the workplace.

A non-union workplace cannot afford instability. It cannot afford a situation where the workers and supervisors are at odds with management in terms of the ongoing operation of the workplace. Uncertainty, conflict and leaders who are out of touch with their people all combine to create a fertile climate for trade union organizing activity.

Change is inevitable, but it should be managed as much as possible. It should become part of the workplace culture. Workers and supervisors should be an integral part of change — they should see themselves as the architects of change and not simply its victims or its opponents. When we talk of having workers "buy in" to change, we do not simply mean that management should be convincing as to the reasons for imposing change. Much better, we should look to the workers to participate in change and to convince themselves that the particular aspects of change are, at best, beneficial and, at worst, neutral to their own well-being in the workplace.

◆
CHAPTER 3

GOOD HUMAN RESOURCES MANAGEMENT AT WORK

To this point, we have introduced the importance of good human resources management, along with the players in the workplace and the legal and other boundaries that dictate the territory in which a Canadian workplace operates. It is time to put these people and these concepts to work. There are five building blocks that we will use on the path to good human resources management:

- Creating a framework
- Communicating expectations
- Correcting, cajoling and compliments — enforcing standards
- Complaints — creating an open atmosphere for questions and criticism
- Continuous renewal and inevitable change

The Framework

Each of these building blocks will be explored in a separate section, but before we get there, it is useful to look at the big picture. The overall goal is to produce goods or to provide services in an efficient and effective manner. Management's operational objectives are to minimize waste and maximize profitability (in the private sector) or relevance and usefulness (in the public sector).

We need people to achieve our objectives. We have already seen that people work for us or with us in many different guises. Our principal focus is on those who work for us as employees and, in particular, those who are workers, or subordinate employees.

As soon as we have people working for us, a significant set of legal concepts springs into play. We have to operate our business or institutional activity subject to the limitations and costs created by these concepts. As a result, we want to understand and shape the concepts in the manner that makes it easiest for us to achieve our goals without undue restriction.

The framework that we create, especially in terms of the phantom collective agreement and the other self-imposed boundaries, should absorb the common law and legal requirements that face us. The law will compel certain aspects of the framework. Other aspects will be what we choose to include — the self-imposed boundaries. We want to achieve a seamless framework, so that there will be little, if any, visible distinction between that which we must do and that which we choose to do in respect of our employees, in pursuit of our business or institutional objectives.

Communication

The elements of the framework, as well as our objectives, must be communicated to our employees in a manner that is simple, straightforward and repetitive. We have to post notices and key concepts. We have to distribute policy booklets that are written for the eyes of our employees and not for the back of a locked cabinet. We have to train on an ongoing and systematic basis.

Communication is a two-way street. An important avenue of communication is the complaint procedure, which merits separate discussion below. The communication that draws our attention here is from the employer to its employees. What are you trying to achieve? How are you trying to achieve it? What are the standards of performance that we expect of our employees, both in terms of quality, quantity, and appropriate conduct?

For the most part and perhaps for all things, excellence is an entirely appropriate standard. You do not have to settle for mere adequacy. It is not enough, however, to want to be excellent. You have to be able to define excellence, to teach it, and to enforce it. Excellence is not a pipe dream; it is hard work. It requires both leadership, in terms of defining a vision and setting targets, and management, in terms of working with employees on a day-to-day basis to do the little things right so that the big things will happen as an inevitable result.

Performance Management

Most of our employees will "get it", almost all of the time. These are the employees who I refer to as able and willing. Some of our employees will resist or refuse or simply be unwilling to achieve at the levels that we require. These are the ones who are able but unwilling. The employees who are able and willing deserve positive reinforcement. When these employees slip up, management has to react, but in a restrained manner that is designed to correct the sub-standard behaviour without creating undue resentment and antagonism. As we will discuss at greater length, significant misconduct requires a more significant response. In extreme cases, a single incident may be sufficient to fracture the employment relationship irreparably. As well, employees who are able but unwilling and who resist or refuse on an ongoing basis, even if each incident is relatively minor, may run out of chances to meet the reasonable standards that are set by management.

Beyond performance issues caused by employee misconduct or neglect, some employees may not "get it", or not often enough, because they may lack the qualifications, training, or intelligence to perform the work at the level that is expected. These are the employees who are willing but unable. Assuming that the established level of performance is achievable, and is being achieved, by other employees, then a management response is required, but it is not suitable to respond in a disciplinary fashion. As we will discuss, there are a range of non-disciplinary responses that are designed to assist these kinds of poor performers, up to and including non-disciplinary demotions or dismissals if required.

There is another kind of performance issue that exists, in addition to bad behaviour and inadequacy. That is the issue created by absenteeism. There are two main branches of the absenteeism problem. One branch is blameless absenteeism, which sometimes means that management cannot prove that the employee was absent without good reason. The other branch is culpable absenteeism, which features elements of misconduct, such as no-calls, no-shows and late arrivals. Sometimes the two branches intertwine, such that the employee is off for a valid reason, but has not called in or communicated with management in the appropriate fashion.

The first branch — blameless absenteeism — has two sub-branches. The first of these is inhabited by unfortunate employees who have long-term debilitating illnesses or injuries, including disabilities that may prevent them from ever returning to their previous position, or to any kind of work. The second sub-branch generally requires more action from management. Here dwell the employees who have repetitive short-term absences, often for a variety of alleged ailments, some of which may be claimed as arising from workplace situations. Disciplinary action is not appropriate for blameless absenteeism, but there are non-disciplinary measures that management has at its disposal, and these often can be used to great effect to improve overall attendance.

Complaints

Many supervisors or managers like to boast about an open-door policy. In some cases, that is delusional thinking. In other cases, it is simply inadequate. One of the key aspects of a collective agreement, which is required by law, is a formal complaints procedure, called the grievance and arbitration procedure. Management in non-union workplaces will find it very difficult to replicate arbitration, which is the system of final and binding third-party adjudication; however, the grievance procedure should be fairly easy to copy, in most significant details.

It is tremendously important to ensure that employees have an effective outlet for complaints. It really does not matter whether or not the complaints are valid. What matters is that the employees have an opportunity to vent, and that management has a wide-open window onto whatever it is that is irritating the workers or any one of them.

Complaints are important in any workplace, but especially in non-union workplaces. The last thing that management would want to see is their employees turning to a third party, a trade union, primarily because they felt that management was not listening to them. Sometimes workplaces become unionized because of low wages and poor benefits. More often, unions will find fertile ground in workplaces that feature insecurity, poor communication and perceived favouritism, even if the compensation package is reasonably good.

Management cannot find out where it is vulnerable unless it is prepared to listen. You have to work at listening. It is not enough to say that you are willing to listen; you have to make it easy for employees to speak out. That requires both a culture of receptive listening and a complaint procedure. In chapter 7, we will explore the complaints process in greater detail, complete with suggested forms and procedures.

Renewal and Change

Nothing stays the same. Nothing lasts forever. Each of us is in a permanent state of change. Together, we are all changing, always. The only thing that you can count on is that you cannot count on anything.

To some extent, you can manage change. To other extents, you simply have to be ready to respond to change. To put this second point into clearer focus, think of any workday over the past few weeks or months. I challenge you to find even a single day when you went into work at the expected time, with a plan for the day, then achieved each part of your plan at the expected time and went home, happy and complete, at a reasonably normal quitting time.

This kind of order rarely happens, if ever. Problems pop up all over the place, and often from entirely unexpected directions. Indeed, with e-mail and voice-mail, many of us now spend the first few minutes of each workday identifying all the surprises that combine to throw off our plan for the day before we have had even our first sip of coffee, tea or juice.

The last thing that I would ever tell you is "don't plan". On the contrary, planning is fundamental to the kind of leadership that I espouse. I will say this — always keep room for the unexpected in your plans. You should never say that your day was thrown completely off balance by some unexpected event. Instead, you should say that, as expected, you had to spend part of your day dealing with the unexpected.

In terms of your ability to manage change, I preach a calendar system, which is reviewed in further detail in chapter 8. For your key areas of human resources policy, like safety, human rights, productivity, technology and absenteeism, pick a month. September, a month of renewed focus, may be safety month. April, when everything is new again, may be human rights month. For most of you, do not bother with the summer months, because too many people are away at any given time, and always avoid the month that is your fiscal year end. That still leaves you with nine months to work with. Safety and human rights are givens — indeed, you may split human rights in two, discrimination and harassment — but there are six or seven months left for other areas that you consider as key to your workplace.

Whatever month you choose for whatever policy, that month should become enshrined for the indefinite future. For example, every December is safety month. Every December, you will review and revise your safety policies and procedures. Every December, you will train your employees and run a communication campaign that features safety issues. That does not mean that you will ignore safety for the rest of the year. With an active safety committee, that would not be possible, and it is not desirable in any event.

What the calendar system ensures is that, whatever else may happen, for at least one month each year, there will be a particular focus on your key areas of human resources policy, such as safety. This will help the organization stay current and avoid the problems faced by many other organizations, when they do not realize how badly out-of-date they are until some serious situation arises. By then, it may be already too late.

CHAPTER 4

CREATING A FRAMEWORK

S o far, we have looked at the big picture. In the course of painting the big picture, many key details have become apparent. As we move into each of the specific areas of good human resources management in a non-union workplace, the intention is to focus on many more specific issues and recommendations. In law and other areas of human endeavour, we often draw the distinction between the forest and the trees. To a great extent, thus far, I have been describing the forest. It is very important to keep the forest, the big picture, always in mind. It is not enough, however, to look only at the big picture. Just as you cannot sit in your office and expect to be effective in managing your people who are engaged in production or providing services, so too you cannot be satisfied with a general knowledge of the forest. You have to get right into it. You have to examine the individual trees and make your own assessment of what is rotten and what is sound. So, off we go, into the woods.

When we go into the woods, it is helpful to know where we are going, what we want to do on the way and once we get there, and how we get back out again. We need a set of objectives. We need to achieve some success quickly to reinforce the positive aspects of the journey. We need direction, both to get to where we want to go and to get back out again.

For the most part, we do not want to start from scratch. We want to find out the extent to which we already have useful elements of the framework. To know just how useful, and to help us identify what is missing, we should look to others who have gone into the same woods or who are in the process of making the same journey. Once we have taken an inventory and measured it, then we are in a position to complete our preparations for the trip.

So, to achieve a framework for good human resources management, the first step is to look at the policies, procedures, rules, practices, culture and history of our organization. We need to engage in a self-audit. We need to perform due diligence on our own organization, as if it were an organization that we might want to acquire and not simply the organization that we already have.

The second step is to look at other organizations that might provide for a useful comparison. This would include related or affiliated plants or offices, organizations within our geographical community or organizations within our industry or area of endeavour. For a non-union organization, it is very useful to find union counterparts. Having identified different comparators, we want to measure ourselves. Do they have pieces that are missing from our organization? Are there other pieces that they have in a different form that might improve on what we currently have? Do we have pieces that they do not have and we do not need, at least not to the extent of the current form? The third step is to improve our framework - organize, modify, add, subtract, and organize again.

What Currently Exists

Every workplace at any stage in its existence, with the possible exception of the very beginning, already has two major repositories of knowledge: paper and people. Let us look at each of those.

There is paper everywhere in a workplace. If as much time was spent reading existing paper as is spent creating new paper, there might be much less paper. For purposes of human resources management, paper comes in two principal varieties. There is the general paper that is meant for the entire workplace - the policies, procedures, rules, notices, lists, health and safety minutes, blank forms and employee booklets (benefits, pensions, orientation and perhaps even phantom agreements in some form or other). There is also the personal paper that lives in the personnel files and medical files (if separate) that should exist for each employee.

There are three exercises that I find very useful in doing a paper audit of a non-union workplace. First, look in our offices and on our bulletin boards. Let us see what we find, in our desks and on our shelves. Is it consistent from supervisor to supervisor? Is it dated? Is it current? Do employees know it? Do they have a copy and, if not, why not? Do we have a distribution list to tell us who got what document and when it was received? What do we have posted and who is responsible for ensuring that required postings are current and in place?

The second exercise is to look in the personnel files. Are the files tidy? Are the documents on some sort of a brad so that they are not loose? Are they in reverse chronological order? Are there meaningful separations, so that medical information is kept apart from other information? Is discipline separate? Are there performance evaluations and, if so, are they regular or haphazard?

The third exercise is to come up with a list of classifications and a pay grid. This can be most telling in a non-union workplace and there are often many unpleasant surprises and inconsistencies. To what extent does seniority or service play a role? Are there merit levels for pay and, if so, how does the employer determine merit levels for each employee? Is there a logical order to the classifications so that work is paid in accordance with its value to the organization? What is the history of pay increases?

It is not enough for you to bury yourself in paper. You have to get to know your people. Part of the HRP's job is to get out to where the workers are on a regular, daily basis. This is even more necessary for supervisors. You need to identify your long-service workers, the natural leaders, the over-achievers and the outsiders. Who are your problem employees, whether in terms of discipline, poor attendance or low skill?

At a higher level, you need to identify how your supervisors are performing, both as a group and on an individual basis. Are they on side? Do they have confidence and the necessary will to administer discipline, enforce standards, and follow the policies, procedures and rules of your workplace? Do they feel empowered or do they fret about a history of perceived and possibly real betrayal by higher levels of management? Are they working with reasonable consistency as a team or are there hard supervisors and soft ones, sowing confusion among the workers and decreasing respect for the management team as a whole? Is the supervisory workload fairly distributed? Do your supervisors play it strictly by the book or do they understand the meaning of discretion and do they exercise reasonable judgement at appropriate times? Do they have an even keel or are they emotional and possibly biased in dealing with their subordinate workers?

You will not get to know your people overnight. You will also not get to know them by accident. You have to make the effort to meet with your people one on one and in groups. You should have a plan for meeting your people and you should set deadlines. When you meet, you have to overcome the tendency to talk to your people and learn to get them to talk to you. The more listening you can do, the more you will learn. This is not a one-off exercise; it is continuous. Once you have met with your people, you have to start to meet them all over again.

Other Models

All organizations have a number of other organizations to which they can compare. In most cases, it is pretty easy to get decent information about how those other organizations manage their human resources. In making such comparisons, you have two complementary objectives. First, you want to organize your own workplace in an effective manner, and you want to offer reasonable and relevant terms and conditions to your workers. Second, you want to minimise the possibility of union organizing at your plant.

Here is what you are looking for:

- Written policies, especially those dealing with human rights issues and safety.
- Employee handbooks and employee orientation manuals.
- Benefits and pension handbooks.
- Wage schedules.
- Procedures, especially complaint procedures, scheduling of work and overtime, attendance management, leave procedures and scheduling vacations.
- Rules, especially setting out disciplinary infractions and safety rules.
- In a unionized workplace, collective agreements.
- Also in a unionized workplace, arbitration decisions and possibly labour relations board decisions.
- In any workplace, wrongful dismissal decisions, and decisions of administrative tribunals dealing with matters of human rights, employment standards, health and safety and workers' compensation; with co-operation from other workplaces, you might also have access to settlements.

Here are some places to look:

- Look at other plants or offices within your own company or organizational structure; or look within associated or related organizations. These are your own people. Perhaps you already receive significant information from them. If not, it should be easy to get information, especially in these days of enhanced electronic transfer of data.

- Look within your community, especially if you are in a smaller town. Smaller communities typically feature a handful of significant industries or public sector employers (such as hospitals, or municipal or county government). The questions to ask yourself are: for whom do my employees' children, parents and spouses work? For whom would my employees work if not with us? Answer those questions and you will know whom to contact for information. Note that information about unionized operations is always pretty easy to get. Collective agreements are not private contracts; they are public documents that are accessible to anyone who wants to take a look. As well, there may be decisions - especially arbitration decisions - that are easy to access. In any event, HRP's are usually quite helpful to each other, as you should be to other HRP's. You can often get as much information as you could reasonably handle, simply by asking for it.

- Be alert to where relatives or friends of your employees are employed. It is often the case that union organizing is started for reasons that have nothing to do with how your business is operating. It simply may be that one of your employees is dating or married to a union steward in another plant.

- Look within your industry, wherever your competitors, suppliers or customers may be located. If you supply product to a unionized company and the same union or a related union attempts to organize your employees, you can expect that they will point to the terms and conditions in place at your unionized customer, especially if there is an argument that they are superior to what is in place at your own plant. In the same way, suppliers who are in a contractual relationship with you may be a reference point for a union organizing campaign. At the same time, and even if there is no union in sight, the companies in your own industry provide an excellent resource for terms and conditions that would be suitable with your employees.

Creating Your New or Improved Framework

Start with the big picture, and then get into the details. Make sure that you give yourself some early successes. You do not have to achieve everything at once. You should not expect that what you achieve will last forever. As long as you are heading in a generally consistent direction, and not swinging about like a weather vane in shifting winds, you should expect to review and revise whatever you achieve on an ongoing basis. Success is achieved step by step, in small increments. Here are some steps you can take in a sequence that makes sense, but is obviously subject to your own current situation and requirements:

1. Separate your employees into groups, such as blue collar, white collar, front line supervisors, middle managers and professionals, and senior executives. Some aspects of human resources management will apply to all groups; other aspects will apply uniquely or differently to individual groups. Once you have different groups identified, you will be able to divide your employees further into sub-groups such that, for your workers in particular, you will be able to identify an existing classification structure.

2. Establish or review and revise your principal policies, such as human rights, safety, attendance management, modified work, confidential employee assistance and job evaluation.

3. Establish or review and revise your principal terms and conditions of employment:
   - hours of work, including scheduling and breaks;
   - relevance of service and seniority to promotions and lay-offs;
   - leaves of absence, including pregnancy leave, parental leave, emergency leave and bereavement leave;
   - vacation entitlement and holidays;
   - wages, including premium pay and overtime;
   - benefits and pension entitlement;
   - perquisites, including paid uniforms and safety equipment (such as footwear and eyeglasses).

4. Establish or review and revise such major procedures as discipline, non-disciplinary warnings for attendance problems, and a procedure for employee complaints.

5. Establish or review and revise such other procedures as:

- bringing human rights concerns to the attention of management and how such concerns will be investigated;
- how safety incidents are to be reported and investigated;
- how workplace accidents or illnesses thought to be caused by the workplace are to be reported and investigated;
- how employees are to return to work following illnesses or injuries – including work trials, work hardening periods;
- dealing with employees who have drug or alcohol abuse issues, and circumstances under which the employer will support rehabilitation programs, including funding;
- how employees who are absent, late, or who want to leave early or for part of the work day are supposed to communicate such absences or requests for short leave to the employer;
- dealing with employees who are incarcerated - whether or not the employer will participate in temporary absence programs, and circumstances under which leaves of absence will be granted;
- how jobs will be evaluated in the event of changes in procedures or equipment - you will want to consider whether or not you have job descriptions; in a manufacturing operation or other operation requiring physical labour, these in turn may be based on physical demands analyses, ergonomic reports, or other work environment reviews;
- how job vacancies will be posted and how employees go about bidding for such vacancies;
- how work will be scheduled and, if there are shifts, whether or not employees will be able to switch shifts with other employees, and how they do that;
- how overtime will be scheduled or assigned and which employees have access to the overtime work;
- how employees apply for leaves of absence, including emergency leave;
- whether or not there will be lieu days or floating holidays that need to be scheduled, and how employees are supposed to do that;
- how employees apply for benefits;
- how employees apply for such perquisites as safety footwear and safety glasses.

6. Establish or review and revise any specific rules that are particular to your operation. Here are some points to remember:

- if your rules are not on one page, get busy editing or reorganizing your rules;
- break your rules into more bite-size pieces;
- add some graphics;
- make sure that there is a consequence clearly identified for breaching a rule;
- never paint yourself into a corner; no consequence should be automatic; you should not force yourself to manage simply "by the book" — management should always retain a discretion to act in a manner that best fits the particular circumstances of any situation; each case is potentially different from every other case.

7. Make sure that you are left with a co-ordinated and cohesive set of materials. Think of your framework as a desktop. You do not want a jumble of paper and files and stuff piled in a haphazard mess that makes sense to nobody else, and possibly not even to you. Instead, you want a tidy desk that someone replacing you could sit behind for the first time and, with a reasonable period of familiarization, your replacement could start to function in a manner consistent with everything that had gone on before.

This tidy desk should be more than an analogy. It should be, in effect, your objective as you create your framework. Whether analogy or reality, here is what your replacement might find on your tidy desk:

- right in the middle of the desk would be a binder of policies, neatly tabbed and indexed, with procedures and forms appended to each policy; the procedures and forms would be created in a manner intended for general distribution and use by workers and other employees; if you are one of those "literal" workplaces that I described with approval in chapter 2 above, you will have an actual phantom collective agreement in the binder and not simply the different elements of that phantom spread throughout your framework;
- off to one side would be a booklet for distribution to employees setting out benefits, pension (if applicable), vacation entitlement, holidays, leave entitlement, perquisites, classifications and a wage structure;
- on the other side would be a set of rules designed for posting in your workplace;

- in your desk drawer would be pads with complaint forms, disciplinary reports, incident reports, job vacancy postings and applications, leave applications, and vacation request forms; some operations may also require time sheets and overtime sheets if this is not handled separately by a payroll group;
- in another desk drawer would be any forms required for government filings, such as workers' compensation forms and records of employment.

Creating Buy-In With Your Management Team and Your Workers

In developing policies, procedures, booklets, rules and forms, and in lining up workplace practices with all of this activity, you should actively seek buy-in throughout the process. To a large extent, this will be a top-down process. Developing booklets and forms is not generally a group activity and somebody has to initiate and drive the process of creating the framework. There remains plenty of opportunity for input, there is a tremendous need for communication and training, and there should be an ongoing process of framework development and renewal. In looking for buy-in, you should have at least three objectives to keep in mind with your management team, your workers and other employees:

1. You want their widespread input before finalizing any policies, procedures and rules because the other players in your workplace might have very good ideas. You never start with a blank slate and there are different stages for gathering input. Presumably you are acting at the outset with a mandate from senior management and with the active participation of at least some of the members of the management team. Once you have a cohesive draft, you then could seek input from the entire management team, front line supervisors in particular. Once you have a completed draft, but prior to implementation, you should consider seeking input from representatives of the workers and other employees. For this purpose, you could have the workers and other employees appoint their own representatives, either on an ongoing basis or for the purposes of this project. Alternatively, you could make the selections yourself, so that you achieve a representative sampling of the employee population.

2. As well as producing good ideas that will improve your framework, input also creates widespread ownership. If only for this purpose, you should actively seek out opportunities to implement some of the suggestions you receive, especially those from the representatives of workers and other employees. A classic negotiating tactic is to give the other side options for settlement. This quite often ends with them debating over which of your options they are prepared to accept, whereas they might have opposed each option if presented separately. In the same way, when developing policies, procedures and rules, you should consider providing your target audiences with alternatives. As soon as they start serious consideration of your alternatives, they will have accepted the framework itself — the rest is simply detail.

    In the ancient civilized world, it used to be said that all roads lead to Rome. My own translation of that, using our analogy of travelling into the forest, is that there are many paths to the clearing in the middle of the forest that is our destination. Your objective is not so much to dictate the path that has to be travelled. Instead, your principal objective is to get everyone headed in the same general direction towards the same destination. If they want to choose their path, especially if it is one of the paths that you suggested in the first place, then they are all the more likely to ensure that the path they have chosen is a good route.

3. Once you have your framework in place, at least in part, you have to promote it actively. As a lesson in what not to do, let us consider a common experience in a unionized workplace. Two negotiating committees work hard to achieve a collective agreement. As is typical, they go through conciliation and are facing the prospect of a work stoppage before a settlement is finally achieved. Then there is a nervous period of a few days while the negotiators wait for completion of the ratification process. Finally, after a close vote, the workers approve the settlement. Then, nothing much happens, other than implementing the increases in the compensation package. It takes forever to produce the new collective agreement. There is no training of front line supervisors and other members of the management team as to the significant changes in the terms and conditions of employment. Indeed, there is no overall review of the agreement itself.

Do not make the same mistake in a non-union workplace. Indeed, you should have a much easier time than the best of the union workplaces. Not only do you have the same opportunity to train your management team, but you also have completely unfettered access to your workers, as well as to other employees. There is no union to run interference or to give a different and possibly distorted message. So get in there. Be prompt and thorough. Promote common understanding between workers and management. Promote consistency within your management team. Make sure that everyone understands his or her role. Make sure that your front line supervisors understand the authority that they have and its limits. Promote the supporting role of the HRP and make it clear that the management of human resources primarily lies with those who are responsible for operational management.

If you do a good job securing buy-in, then you will be well on the way to communicating your expectations, both to the management team and to the rest of the workforce.

Gaining Input while Maintaining Control

Input is important. Buy-in at different levels is important in developing an effective framework. In securing input and creating buy-in, HRP's should continue to focus on two key points:

1. Although many may participate, someone, or a small group of people, has to drive the process. It is up to the HRP to create or oversee directly the preparation of the initial draft of any documents that are part of the framework. The HRP must oversee revisions and ensure that any input receives a prompt response. The HRP must set an overall timeframe, with interim targets; otherwise, projects will suffer the fate of so many good intentions and trail off into nothing.

2. Simply because input is received does not mean that it has to be implemented. Management must retain ultimate control. Management has the final say in respect of the framework. Input that is not consistent with management's vision cannot be incorporated into the framework.

   At the same time, if you are serious about input and you convince your employees that the input process is important, then you will create expectations that should be met. The way to balance the need to maintain control with the importance of gaining input is to manage the input process. Here are some tactics:

- rather than firing off draft documents and requesting feedback, focus the input; make the process "user-friendly"; take different segments of a policy or a procedure and ask employees to respond to specific questions;
- as was discussed in the previous section, about creating buy-in, provide employees with options, so that they are selecting between alternatives that already have been determined to be acceptable to management;
- use discussion groups, which have the effect of gathering input and training the employees at the same time;
- use questionnaires and surveys;
- avoid pride of authorship — if you receive a suggestion that is worded differently or framed differently, but seems just as effective, consider deferring to the input instead of the original draft;
- provide feedback to employees about the input received, including explanations as to why certain ideas have not been incorporated into the framework;
- thank employees for the input received, even if it is not used, and look for ways to give it value — for example, "even though your idea was not accepted, it caused us to think about this other aspect of the policy and to make the following additional changes";
- follow through — employees who take the time to make suggestions or to respond to inquiries do not necessarily expect that their views will be incorporated into the framework; however, they certainly expect something to happen.

Once you invite your employees to participate in the process of developing a framework, which includes the ongoing process of review and revision, do not abandon them. Management continues to be the ultimate decision-maker. As such, management has decided to involve employees in the process. Do not betray your own decision to create participation.

If you open the door, only to ignore your invited guests, then you will find that you have pushed your employees further away than if you had not bothered to consult them in the first place. As discussed throughout this section, there are many ways to shape the input process and to demonstrate that you value the input received and, at the same time, to achieve the kind of framework that you consider to be consistent with operational objectives.

◆

CHAPTER 5

COMMUNICATING EXPECTATIONS

Once you have established a basic framework, you have to be both skilled and diligent in communicating your expectations to the human resources you intend to manage. Remember that management has the right to organize the workplace and to set and enforce the standards for performance and acceptable conduct. Your framework provides a basic structure, but organizing a workplace and achieving standards are ongoing activities. To avoid a communications breakdown, here are the groups that you have to focus on and how you should approach each group:

Higher Level Management

To support the effective management of an organization's human resources, higher-level management has to travel in two directions. In one direction, higher-level management has to be fully involved. In the other direction, they have to stay out of the way. Although these may seem to be contradictory tasks, they are harmoniously achieved at different levels and at different stages in the process.

We will start with staying out of the way. Front-line supervisors and the second-level managers to whom they directly report have day-to-day responsibility for human resources management. Higher-level management has to support that responsibility at every turn. I have seen operations where that lesson has been forgotten or never learned. The result is that workers ignore their immediate supervisors and, with the blind concurrence of senior management, the supervisors are effectively marginalized. If there are new practices to implement, the workers will confirm their validity with senior management. If there is corrective action to hand out or if performance is to be evaluated, it will be ignored or resisted unless and until senior management validates it. If there are complaints, even of a fairly trivial nature, they cannot be settled without the intervention of senior management.

This is very destructive to the management team. It is a waste of money and a waste of supervisory talent. It is a waste of senior management's time. But it is even worse than that. Front-line supervisors bad-mouth senior management, perhaps without always realizing what they are doing. If workers complain about policies, procedures, rules or new practices, supervisors might retort, "we are just doing what we are told" or "take it up with the management", seemingly in ignorance of the fact that they are or should be part of the management team. For their part, without sufficient hands-on knowledge of the day-to-day operations or the workers, senior management often make poor decisions that are designed more to avoid disputes than to support the framework of human resources management. Decisions that get the product out or keep up a high level of delivery of services in the short-run may be very damaging in the long-term, or perhaps much sooner than that.

Here is where it should be clear that any reference to HRP's as support staff is not intended to suggest, in any way, that HRP's are somehow minor players. By contrast, HRP's have to be strong, knowledgeable, committed, and more than a little stubborn. It is up to the HRP to ensure that supervisors feel that they are included in the management team and to ensure that all supervisors have bought in to the program to the extent that they treat it as their own program. In such an environment, workers who have complaints will be met by supervisors who are eager to explain and support whatever part of the framework has generated the complaint. More important, such supervisors will be eager to resolve the complaint at the earliest possible opportunity and in the most effective manner possible.

It is also up to the HRP to ensure that senior management is fully informed and has the opportunity to be fully involved in the big picture. Senior management should, for the most part, be able to avoid the nuts and bolts of human resources management. In addition to the overall framework itself, senior management should be involved only in particularly serious situations or if a complaint cannot be resolved at an early level.

Indeed, in this respect, the most important understanding that the HRP can forge with senior management is the extent to which they are prepared to delegate authority to front-line and/or second-line supervisors. This is especially true in terms of disciplinary authority, but stretches to all areas where management has discretionary decision-making power. It is unhealthy to give away all authority but, within limits, supervisors should be given as much autonomy and as much decision-making authority as they can reasonably handle.

Front-Line Supervisors

Front-line supervisors fulfil a key function in the management of any workplace. The responsibility for effective human resources management falls most directly on their shoulders. The success of the policies of management — whether for work production, safety or employee relations — will be determined, to a large extent, by the day-to-day actions of the supervisors. In some situations, the actions of an individual supervisor may have far-reaching implications for the whole organization. It is, therefore, an ongoing responsibility of HRP's and senior management to ensure that front-line supervisors have the training and support that is necessary for them to manage effectively. Supervisors who know what they are doing, and who trust the rest of the management team to back them up in their efforts, will have the tools necessary to be workplace leaders.

Here are the three biggest messages to deliver consistently to your supervisors:

- the supervisors must follow the framework, as individuals and collectively as a group — there should be plenty of opportunity for input when the framework is first established and when it is reviewed, modified and renewed thereafter, but in the meantime the framework should be respected; it is more than a mere guideline;
- consistency is key — each supervisor has to be consistent as an individual on a day-to-day basis; as well, the members of the management team have to be consistent with each other and supportive of each other;
- the decisions that supervisors make matter; and their decision making authority, within limits, will be supported by senior management; however, both to maintain consistency and to promote harmony among the workers, supervisors have to understand that support for supervisors will be neither blind nor universal.

Following the Framework

The rules for following the framework are essentially the same rules that should be preached to supervisors in a unionized workplace, where supervisors have to operate within the restrictions imposed by a collective agreement:

1. Be thoroughly familiar with the framework and how it dovetails with labour and employment legislation and with the requirements and expectations of the employer:
   - get help from human resources, your colleagues or your boss if you do not understand the framework or the law;
   - give employees what they are entitled to receive; and
   - do not expand the framework through loose or inconsistent application.

2. The framework decides what is "fair"; the framework is not subject to individual application either by a supervisor or towards workers; a supervisor should be neither a soft touch nor a taskmaster and should not create the perception or the reality of preferential treatment.

3. The framework is a limitation on management rights, even though it is self-imposed; interpret ambiguous or generally worded provisions in management's favour.

4. Know management's position on contentious issues or ambiguous provisions.

5. Management acts; the workers react; do not compromise your authority; do not share your responsibility for interpreting and applying the framework with your workers.

6. Supervisors will have discretionary powers in many situations; your discretion always should be exercised in a manner that is not arbitrary, not discriminatory, but reasonable and in good faith.

7. Ensure that your workers are promptly and clearly notified of any changes in the framework and any changes in practice that you are implementing.

8. Consider your actions and justify your decisions within the context of the framework and operational requirements; always consider the impact that your actions or your application of the framework will have on the entire organization.

Consistency

Nothing destroys the framework faster than inconsistent application. Consistency is easy to preach, but not so easy to practise. Here are three key aspects:

1. Each supervisor has to be internally consistent. Nobody is a machine. There will always be workers who rub you the wrong way and other workers who are easy to assist even when they are not achieving your standards. You will have good days, better days, and days to forget. That is the beauty of a good framework. As part of the management team, you have helped to develop the policies, procedures and rules that will frame your day-to-day practices with little regard to who you are dealing with and how you are feeling about it or, indeed, how you are feeling in general. This is not so much managing by the book. Rather, it is managing on a solid and comprehensive foundation, with the limitations or boundaries clearly understood.

2. You have to avoid the reality and the perception of playing favourites. Applying behavioural standards should not vary depending on a worker's job performance in terms of quality and quantity. High performers can be directly rewarded for that, but they should have to meet the same standards of conduct as other workers. In the same way, employees who are models of good behaviour still have to meet the standards set for quality and quantity of output. Some workers can be like children, with antennae especially tuned to any kind of imbalance in treatment.

Do not let your enthusiasm for fairness carry you away. There are at least three common traps that you should avoid:

- Your goal is equitable treatment, not equal treatment. You are managing human beings, not solving mathematical problems. There are no perfect answers and there are no perfect systems of comparison between different people.
- Your focus should be on process, not results. Results will likely differ for different people in different circumstances. The framework, along with consistent practice, should provide both the appearance and the reality of equitable treatment in terms of your approach to different employees in similar situations.

- You are entitled to reward employees who exceed standards, just as you are obligated to assist employees who are falling short. Indeed, you may have a legal obligation to assist employees whose shortcomings are attributable, at least in part, to a disabling condition. The key, whether with rewards or assistance, is that there should be a direct link and, for the most part, the link should be broadcast in advance. For example, if it is part of your wage structure to pay high-achieving employees a merit premium, then higher pay is the result for superior performance, and not leniency in applying the absenteeism policy or preference in scheduling vacations. As another example, an employee who is disabled should be entitled to accommodation, but not preferential rights to a promotion without regard to the service or qualifications of other employees.

3. Each supervisor and each member of the management team has to strive to be consistent with every other member of the team. Naturally, there will be different styles and different strengths. Those differences are no excuse for ignoring the framework, making things up as you go along or simply failing to do what you should be doing in order to avoid conflict. The goal is relative consistency, not absolute equality of treatment between supervisors. Indeed, nobody has all the right answers and each supervisor can be both student and teacher at different times in interaction with the rest of the management team.

Here again the HRP has a key role to play. Understanding, observing and assessing the different supervisory styles is necessary to achieve and maintain a balanced approach to all of the people working in your operation. Some supervisors need to be toned down and others need to be pushed, prodded or pulled into more activity. Every supervisor I have ever met has benefitted from ongoing communication about the expectations of the organization, as well as regular training in human resources management.

Workers

Communication with the workers occurs in at least five ways:

1. *Distribution of paper.* This has been discussed at length already in terms of the development of the framework. What is important to

remember is that the paper is more important to the members of management who developed it than it is to the workers who are the recipients. You cannot assume that they will value the paper like you do. You have to create the value. You have to hammer away at its importance. You should get employees to sign for whatever is handed to them, and you should be clear as to your expectations about retention. If it is to be retained in the workplace, you should perform an occasional audit. If it can be retained at home, you may ask that it be brought in from time to time for your review. You should make retention easy, with solid covers or binders in which the paper can be safely stored. You have to be prepared to hand out replacement copies. You have to plan to hand out revisions on a regular basis, likely every two or three years. As part of your training, you should test employees on their knowledge of different aspects of the framework.

2. *General communication and training.* Whether in one-off assemblies of the entire work force or through formal training programs, you will likely deal with your workers on an operations-wide basis in respect of certain aspects of the framework.

3. *Work group communication and training.* However your work force is organized, it likely will feature smaller groups that are led by a supervisor. Depending on the needs of your operations and on the closeness of supervision, these employees may meet together on a daily or weekly basis. At the very least opportunities should be created on a regular basis every couple of weeks for the sharing of information.

4. *Individual and situational communication.* Through corrective action or performance evaluation, both informally and formally, on a regular basis or as needed, each individual worker will receive direct communication that relates to what that particular worker is doing.

5. *Informal communication — the rumour mill.* You cannot stop the rumour mill. You cannot effectively control what employees say to each other. What you have to do is to try to stay plugged in, set up your own network to counteract the negative impacts of the rumour mill, and react in a more formal way when the rumour mill threatens to get out of hand. Remember not to overreact. This is a natural part of any human gathering. Although rumours can be

very harmful, they often can be relatively benign and allow your people to let off some steam.

Other Workplace Players

For the purposes of this book, I have tried to maintain a distinction between workers and other workplace players, who are considered at some length in chapter 1. They include professionals, confidential employees and third parties. In large measure, that distinction is important because it marks out the targets for union organization.

Different groups should not lead to multiple frameworks. All workplace players, regardless of how they are grouped, should be subject to the same framework, at least in terms of the applicable parts, and most parts should be generally applicable. Even third parties need to know "the rules of the road", although they are not subject to any of the aspects of compensation that apply to employees, and are not managed, disciplined or evaluated in a traditional way.

You will have to tailor your framework to the different sections of your audience, but the general rule is to apply as much of it to as many of the workplace players in as many situations as possible. To the extent that it is applied, it should be communicated at least that much and possibly more. There is rarely much harm in providing too much information. It is always a deficiency not to provide enough information or to provide the information, but not often enough.

Communication is a Two-way Street

Although most of our attention has been on communications from the management team to workers and other workplace players, most readers will be keenly aware that communication goes both ways. In chapter 4, we have talked about the importance of input, both for the value of the information received and for the inherent value of creating buy-in to the framework. In chapter 7 we will look at a particular system of receiving information from employees through a complaint procedure that equates to a unionized grievance procedure. Beyond this, it is important for HRP's to reinforce continually with front-line supervisors and all members of the management team that there is no replacement to active listening to all workplace players. The first awareness of big problems may come from very quiet and minor suggestions or complaints from workers.

Here are some specific suggestions for active listening in the workplace:

- You have to be regularly available on the shop floor, in the office area, or on the road, where employees actually work; you have to be in the employee's normal work environment in order to hear what they are trying to communicate.
- Trust is difficult to acquire; it can be lost in a single incident. To be effective as a listener, you have to be trusted by your workers. If you are told something in confidence, the confidence must be respected. If law or policy means that you cannot maintain confidentiality (such as with an allegation of sexual harassment or unsafe work practices), then the employee must be advised, with an explanation, that you have overriding obligations as a supervisor.
- Language barriers or a lack of sophistication on the part of employees can garble the message, but should not diminish its importance; make a special effort to listen to employees who are difficult to understand.
- What you are actually told may not be the real problem. Active listening requires probing; use focused, open-ended questions to get to the bottom of the real issue.
- Sometimes the workers who irritate you the most are the ones to whom you have to listen most closely.
- It is hard to listen when you are talking.
- Listen first, talk second; an employee may be uncomfortable making a suggestion or raising a concern when you have already made your point.
- Follow up. You may not get the full story the first time around.
- If you tell the employee that you will follow up, make sure that you do so. Give the employee a time frame, then be timely in your follow-up. If you need more time, make sure that you advise the employee of the delay.

◆

CHAPTER 6

ENFORCING STANDARDS

H aving set standards and communicated your expectations to your people, you have to measure continuously whether or not your standards are being met. To a great extent, you will work with the entire group. Ultimately, what matters is the performance of the entire team. Remember that the team is made up of individuals. In certain areas, some of your individuals will perform above the standards that you have set, whether in terms of quality, quantity, or both. Excellence should be recognized and rewarded. This may be as simple as a "thank you" and "well done" or it may involve creative and sophisticated incentive or merit pay schemes. However you do it, you know, or you will find out, that standards are subject to being enforced with the carrot as well as with the stick.

Unfortunately, whatever you do, some individuals will fail to meet your standards at least some of the time. If this is happening often, with many of your employees, then there may be a problem with your standards, your communication, or the skills and qualifications of your workers. If this is happening with some of your employees, but not with most others, then the problem is with the individual employee. This may be a disciplinary problem, in that the employee is failing to work at the level of his/her skill and ability. Or, the problem may be non-disciplinary, in that the employee wants to meet your standards, but is simply incapable of doing so.

We will look at four different ways of enforcing standards. Performance evaluations and merit pay each will receive a relatively brief mention. Most of our attention will be on a disciplinary system that I call the corrective action plan, with some time spent at the end on the distinct issue of non-disciplinary action.

Performance Evaluations

Performance evaluations are usually a pain and rarely done well. Used properly, evaluations can be a very effective management tool. Here are eight suggestions:

75

1. *Probationary Employees.* Employers should apply probationary periods in most cases, although it may not be appropriate for senior or exceptionally qualified employees. It should be a standard requirement that performance evaluations be done as part of any probationary period. In some cases, evaluations might be done every few weeks, in accordance with a pre-set schedule. A probationary period should be three months long in the normal case and may be extended for more senior or sophisticated positions. The length of the probationary period should be set out in a written employment contract or hire letter that should be signed off before a new employee actually commences employment. An employee's entitlements if not successful with the probationary period (such as immediate dismissal or dismissal with some amount of termination pay) should also be spelled out and should be checked with the relevant employment standards legislation.

   It is bad enough that some employers do not take advantage of probationary periods at all. Worse still are those who have a probationary period, but fail to evaluate new employees properly. It is a sad case when a negative evaluation is completed after the probationary period has finished — sometimes only by a matter of days or weeks, but still too late as a matter of contract. In other cases, there is no evaluation and yet a determination is made some time after the probationary period that the employee is unsatisfactory. That can be an expensive delay in decision-making.

   In some cases, employees are dismissed before the probationary period has expired, but without the benefit of a proper evaluation. That is the kind of arbitrary and unreasonable decision-making that leads to legal claims based on allegations of bad faith or even discrimination. It is simply inadequate from the standpoint of human resources management and should be avoided.

2. For employees who have passed the probationary period, evaluations should be done on an annual basis. The employer should pick the same time period each year, somewhat in advance of a decision about compensation increases, which also should be determined at the same time for all employees in most cases. It is up to the HRP to monitor the process and to ensure that

evaluations are completed. The support of senior management is obviously very helpful.

3. Technology can be usefully applied to ease the burden of completing performance evaluations. Some organizations are now completing evaluations using an internal web form.

4. Employees should be required to complete a self-evaluation in advance of the supervisor's evaluation. This can be a very effective tool that can also ease the burden of the evaluation.

5. The evaluation should look forward as well as backward. Goals should be set and part of the following year's evaluation should be based on the extent to which the previous year's goals were achieved.

6. Performance evaluations tend to be completed with a ranking of at least average or higher. HRP's should be vigilant to ensure that real evaluations are being done and that meaningful distinctions are drawn between different levels of performance and behaviour.

7. Employees who are having trouble should be put on a monitoring program with periodic interim evaluations completed according to a pre-set schedule — typically on a quarterly basis.

8. In every case, a supervisor should be required to meet with an employee whom s/he has evaluated, in order to explain the evaluation and listen to the employee's feedback. An employee should have an opportunity to add his or her own comments to the evaluation form.

Merit Pay

It is very difficult in a unionized operation to pay on any basis other than in accordance with a classification structure, with some recognition given to improvements in performance that are normal over the first few years of service in each classification. In such cases, where the first few years of service bring increases within a classification, they are usually automatic and do not depend on the actual performance of an employee.

A non-union workplace has a significant advantage and can implement a true merit pay system. Naturally, the starting point is to have a proper wage grid. This is what a wage grid might look like in a manufacturing operation, with five classifications:

Classification	Probation	Start	1 year	2 years	Merit 1	Merit 2
General Lab.	$10.50	$11.00	$11.50	$12.00	$12.50	$13.00+
Operator	$12.50	$13.00	$13.50	$14.00	$14.50	$15.00+
Ship/Receive	$13.50	$14.00	$14.50	$15.00	$15.50	$16.00+
Set Up	$14.50	$15.00	$15.50	$16.00	$16.50	$17.00+
Skilled	$18.50	$19.00	$19.50	$20.00	$20.50	$21.00+

There are a few common features, which I recommend, but which obviously are not fixed in stone and are entirely subject to the particular characteristics of each workplace:

- There is an initial pay raise after completion of the probationary period.
- The standard top rate is the 2-year rate. If an employee moves to the next higher classification, then s/he would go to the probationary rate for that classification, unless s/he was in receipt of merit pay, in which case s/he would go to the start rate or the next higher rate, depending on the amount of merit pay that had been received. Naturally, the merit pay would be lost with the promotion.
- The rates are fixed, and should be followed for the most part, to avoid perceived favouritism, although the second merit rate allows for discretion (which could mean a number of additional merit levels, although it could easily get out of hand). I have used the "+" sign in the above chart to show the potential for discretion at the highest merit level.
- There is no need to start a qualified worker at the probationary rate, especially for higher rated classifications where the probationary rate may not be high enough to get a skilled applicant to accept employment. Again, care should be taken so that exceptions do not become the norm, making the wage grid pointless.

Here are two points that might not be obvious:

- General increases still should take place on an annual basis and would apply across the wage grid. Careful consideration should be given to whether increases should be flat rate increases, which are easily understood by workers, but would shrink the relative difference between steps on the grid and between classifications. The alternative, which maintains the differences, is to have percentage increases across the board. It is possible to give different increases to different classifications, although that could lead to employee resentment.

- When a wage grid is first established, often there can be significant problems fitting current pay rates into a model grid. This can be solved with patience and creativity. I have often used red circles, yellow circles and green circles to help get everyone sorted out. Red circles freeze an employee at his or her current rate until the classification catches up. Green circles freeze the differential between the current rate and the classification rate. Yellow circles are in-between and shrink the differential over time, typically a period of two or three years.

Corrective Action Plan ("CAP")

The implementation and administration of a corrective action plan ("CAP") or system of discipline can be a difficult and unpleasant responsibility. Certainly, it can be the most obvious aspect of the management team's relationship with workers.

The purpose of a CAP is to provide management with a system to help maintain the workplace rules and the standards of behaviour and performance that are considered to be necessary to ensure the orderly and efficient conduct of the employer's business. The rules and standards must be job-related or have a solid operational and business basis. They must be fully communicated to the workforce or generally understood as normal community standards. The workforce must also know that failure to conform to the standards or to obey the rules in the workplace will lead to corrective action at a level that will be determined by the employer to be appropriate on consideration of all relevant facts and circumstances.

At the risk of being obvious, CAP only works if there is something that can be corrected. If an employee is doing his or her best, but simply lacks the qualifications, skill, ability (including physical ability) or intelligence to perform the job at the required standard, then the best CAP in the world is not going to be much help. There are other actions that can and should be taken, but they are not in the nature of a disciplinary system. We will consider this further below at page 94.

If there is something to correct, it is important that the employer should be committed to taking appropriate action. If a supervisor is not prepared to enforce adherence to a rule or standard, s/he is condoning its contravention, and so too is the entire management team.

Discipline is supposed to be corrective in nature, which is why I suggest calling the disciplinary system a CAP. Discipline should not be punitive. Employers are not meant to be the moral conscience of their employees, they are simply meant to achieve the performance that management considers to be necessary in order to achieve operational objectives. In essence, the purpose of the CAP is to help create more efficient and more effective employees, for the benefit of the organization and for the benefit of the employees themselves. Most importantly, the CAP is designed to encourage employees to perform at the standards established by management. The primary purpose should not be to create a paper trail to justify a dismissal for cause, although that may be the result if the employee does not improve performance in response to the corrective actions that are taken.

CAP Fundamentals

The CAP is based on a fundamental principle of minimum force, which means that the employer should take the least serious corrective action thought necessary in order to achieve the objective of appropriate behaviour or improved performance. In this way, corrective action is also progressive. When an employee persists in inappropriate behaviour or poor performance following corrective action, then the original action was not sufficiently strong. As a result, progressively more severe corrective sanctions are imposed in order to reinforce management's concern, as well as to provide the employee with ample opportunity to improve before the final act of dismissal.

Here is what a typical CAP might look like for an employee who continues to violate the safety policy and the procedures established under that policy:

Step 1: oral warning with memorandum to file (although an oral warning is a step up from oral counselling, this still may be insufficient for a safety violation)

Step 2: written warning

Step 3: one-day suspension without pay

Step 4: three-day suspension without pay

Step 5: five-day suspension without pay and final warning

Step 6: dismissal for just cause, without notice, pay in lieu of notice or any other termination pay.

There are a few points that bear noting from the above:

- depending on the seriousness of the infraction, you would not have to start at Step 1 and you could skip a step; indeed, the most serious infractions could lead directly to a dismissal;
- I recommend that suspensions be without pay; it is preferable if you make this clear in the CAP policy itself, which should be brought to the attention of new employees;
- an employee could sue for wrongful dismissal, but an employer's defence is made much stronger if it uses a CAP such as the one above.
- Step 5 could be omitted or it could be an optional step, in which case the final warning would be at Step 4.

Many workplaces would find it helpful to create a CAP form, such as the example on the following page:

[Employer logo]

CORRECTIVE ACTION PLAN

*Name of employee:*_____ *Date:*_____

*Description of incident:*_____

_____

_____

*Applicable standard(s) or rule(s):*_____

_____

_____

*Date and level of prior corrective action:*_____

_____

_____

*Corrective action in this case:*_____

*Date/shift of return to work (if applicable):*_____

This corrective action will remain on your record for two years and will be removed after that time, provided that no other corrective action is required in the meantime. OR

This corrective action will remain on your record indefinitely.

Please be advised that further situations that require corrective action could lead to more severe levels of corrective action up to and including dismissal for cause.

Please contact your supervisor if you have any questions.

*Signature of Supervisor/Manager:*_____ *Date:*_____

*Name and Position of Supervisor/Manager:*_____

***I have received and read this corrective action:*_____**

Employee's Signature

CAP Levels

The six steps from the above example can be collapsed into four basic CAP levels:

1. *Oral counselling, followed by an oral reprimand or warning:*
   - Oral counselling normally is used for a first offence or where the facts and circumstances indicate that more severe CAP levels are not warranted, such as when a normally punctual employee arrives late for work.
   - Oral counselling sometimes is thought of as a kinder, gentler form of oral warning. It is typically one on one and often very brief. In the best meetings, the worker would be invited to recommend a solution for the problem.
   - A cautionary note: supervisors should never have one-on-one meetings with employees behind closed doors, unless the office is a windowed office, and especially if the employee is of the other gender. In an oral warning session, it is good form in any event to have a second member of the management team in attendance.
   - Although no official notice of the incident is placed on the employee's file, the supervisor should retain some form of record for future reference in the event the employee does not correct the sub-standard behaviour — a simple note should do, recording the employee's name, the date of the discussion and a brief summary of what took place.
   - If the supervisor uses some kind of form or a memorandum to file, especially following a more formal meeting to deliver an oral warning, then a copy should be provided to the employee (this is sometimes referred to as a "written verbal").

2. *Written Reprimand or Warning:*
   - A written warning normally is issued when the oral counselling or warning has not elicited the improvement required of the employee and another infraction of the rule has occurred. Therefore, reinforcement of the warning is required. It may also be issued for a first offence that warrants a sanction more severe than an oral reprimand, such as breaching a relatively minor safety rule, or a heated verbal altercation with a co-worker.

A written warning should document at least the following five points:

- briefly describe the misconduct (follow the standard tools of reporting — who, what, why, when and where);
- identify the standard or rule that was breached;
- list any prior warnings;
- indicate the corrective action selected (i.e. written warning); and
- warn of the consequences of continuing or repeating the behaviour: that further corrective action would follow, up to and including dismissal.

One copy of the warning goes to the employee; a second copy is retained on file.

3. *Suspension without Pay:*
   - A suspension without pay is normally imposed when an employee persists in unsatisfactory conduct or behaviour, even after repeated efforts by management to have the employee correct the sub-standard performance. A suspension also may be imposed for a first occurrence of a serious act of misconduct, such as fighting on the job, insubordinate behaviour, and more serious safety infractions. Written confirmation of the suspension should be provided to the employee in much the same form as a written warning; a second copy is retained on file.
   - I suggest using odd-numbered suspensions of one day, three days or five days. That way, if the employee complains about the severity of the suspension and additional mitigating facts are identified, then you could roll back the corrective action without having to return to the prior level of corrective action taken. A progressive CAP could repeat a level, but it should never go backward and generally it should go forward, especially once you are at the level of suspension.
   - I see little point in a suspension that is longer than five days. Unless there are special circumstances, or you are agreeing to reinstate an employee, subject to time served, five days (perhaps even three days) should be plenty as the most serious

corrective action short of dismissal, especially when combined with a clear final warning.

4. *Dismissal*:

The following discussion about dismissal is entirely within the context of the CAP. As such, it contemplates two kinds of situations:

- The first kind of CAP situation arises from progressive discipline, in which a final incident, combined with a record of prior discipline, is justification for dismissal of an unsatisfactory employee.
- The second kind of CAP situation is a single incident discharge arising from a particularly serious act of misconduct.

Chapter 2 explored different aspects of claims for wrongful dismissal, which arise from terminations of employment that are not for cause. There also was reference in chapter 2 to a frustration of contract, when an employee is unable to continue in employment, usually due to a disabling condition. We will summarize these various kinds of dismissal situations at page 94 below, following the review of the CAP.

Here are the key points that deal with dismissal under the CAP:

- The dismissal of the employee normally will take place after all efforts at correcting poor behaviour or sub-standard performance have failed. In some cases, the act of misconduct is of such a serious nature that management feels that it is left with no other option. In those cases, a dismissal for cause may issue, even though it is a first offence. Some examples include a serious breach of trust, such as theft or fraud, or where an employee physically assaults a manager or attacks another employee with a tool or weapon.
- In a non-union workplace, there is a very small risk that an employee could try to argue that an unpaid suspension amounts to a constructive dismissal, and there is a somewhat larger risk that there could be a statutory breach somewhere along the line. Those risks aside, for the most part, the only real likelihood of a legal claim is at the point of dismissal. As a result, until the very end, a non-union employer is almost unfettered in its use of a CAP.
- With freedom comes responsibility. To avoid alienating the workforce, a CAP has to be administered in a consistent and reasonable manner. Individual decisions to correct behaviour

or performance must not be arbitrary, discriminatory, or motivated by bad faith. Given the importance of perception in applying such a system, an employer must strive to appear fair and balanced in its approach.

- As would be usual for any step of the CAP, when imposing dismissal, the decision-maker and another member of the management team should meet with the employee to inform him or her of the action taken and the reasons for it. Written confirmation also should be delivered to the employee, using the format first described above for a written warning; a copy of the letter should be placed on the file.

- As an alternative to dismissal, or as a possible settlement, you may consider continuing employment or reinstating an employee subject to conditions, which also may include a monitoring period.

When Corrective Action is Appropriate

As noted above, there is no point in taking corrective action at all unless there is something to correct. As subsequently discussed, if there is a decision to take corrective action, then there are four basic levels that could apply and at least a couple of different steps at each of the first level of oral counselling or warning, and the third level of unpaid suspensions. The employer's response to a first offence may vary according to the seriousness of the misconduct. Similarly, where an employee has received corrective action previously, the facts and circumstances of a current incident may indicate that more serious corrective action is warranted than simply proceeding to the next step.

Unless penalties for breaches of established rules and standards are specified by the employer's policies, procedures or rules, decisions regarding the appropriate level of corrective action always will involve a degree of subjectivity. In the pursuit of consistency, you will want to minimize this inevitable subjectivity through a suitable investigation of the facts and circumstances of each case. Keep in mind that we are not talking about anything like a criminal investigation, except in those situations where there has been something like theft or assault, in which case the police may become involved in any event. Those exceptions aside, usually we are talking about simple workplace misconduct — a failure to meet standards. For the most part, the processes of investigation and decision-making should be straightforward and prompt — usually a matter of hours or days.

As well as any policies, procedures or rules you may have regarding appropriate levels of discipline, there is one particular situation where the level of corrective action may be pre-determined. If an employee is subject to a serious suspension or is given another chance through reinstatement to the workplace following a dismissal, that should be accompanied by a formal settlement that includes terms and conditions for continued employment or for reinstatement. This is often the case with non-disciplinary absenteeism situations (further considered at page 95 below), as well as in situations that involve substance abuse. Each set of terms and conditions will be based on individual facts, but plans for ongoing employment should have at least these features:

- A threshold requirement to go through rehabilitation in substance abuse cases.
- A requirement for ongoing medical treatment and reporting and, in substance abuse cases, post-rehabilitation care (such as group meetings, like AA).
- A requirement to avoid the originating problem (such as drinking or failing to take prescribed medication to control a permanent condition).
- A requirement to follow applicable attendance procedures.
- A minimum time period, typically two years and subject to extension.

Failure to follow the above features could result in dismissal for cause without further notice. In this way, an alcoholic who goes through a rehabilitation program would be subject to termination, not for the alcoholism (which is a disability covered by human rights provisions), but for choosing to violate the terms and conditions of ongoing employment, which is misconduct.

Although very effective, these "last chance" agreements may run afoul of human rights legislation if not carefully drafted. This is one of the situations where the assistance of an employment lawyer could be very worthwhile.

There are three basic steps in making a decision about corrective action. All three steps are derived from the expectation that management will be responsible for establishing the facts of the case and, if there is a legal proceeding, then management will have the onus of proof, either as a matter of law or as a matter of evidence, depending on the proceeding. Here are the steps:

- Has the employer been able to establish what happened, as a matter of fact? If so, is the employer in a position to identify the employee who may be at fault?
- Is any corrective action warranted? Did the employee engage in misconduct? Could the employee have done something different or better had s/he wanted to or had a better choice been made, when such choice was readily available to the employee?
- If some corrective action is warranted, what is most appropriate, in consideration of the principles of minimum force and progressive action?

Conducting an Investigation

If it seems appropriate, you should investigate cases of misconduct or sub-standard performance promptly and completely. You should try to stay objective. Keep an open mind. Make your decisions at the end of the investigation. Try to avoid investigating simply to support decisions you made right at the outset.

Each employee is responsible for his or her own actions and behaviour. Employees must not be disciplined randomly. You cannot punish the entire workforce simply because you are unable to identify the culprit. Responsibility is determined by the facts identified in the investigation. In gathering facts required for the decision steps set out above, always follow the W5 rule, as per this diagram:

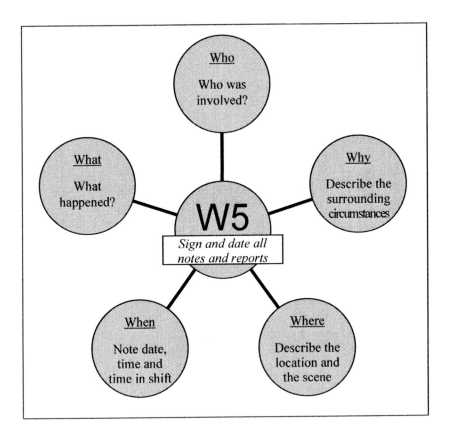

Here are key sources for your facts:

1. Statements of witnesses with direct knowledge of the incident or misconduct, whether as participants or spectators.
2. Statements of persons who were not witnesses, but who have reliable second-hand information. This would be called "hearsay" in a legal proceeding, but is quite useful in a workplace investigation, provided that you remember to treat it as "second-best" information.

3. Documentation pertaining to the misconduct, whether pre-existing or created in the normal course of business at the time of, or shortly following, the incident.
4. Other kinds of evidence, including photographs, videotape, diagrams, and objects.
5. Indirect or circumstantial evidence that should stand up to the following tests:
   - it should point to the employee as having committed the offence or misconduct; and
   - it should exclude any other reasonable explanation, such as a determination that another employee could have committed the offence as easily.

Here are three key points about the investigation process:
1. At the end of every investigation, the employee who has been identified as the target for corrective action should be interviewed, even if s/he has been interviewed earlier in the process. Two points are important to understand:
   - the point of the interview is to provide the employee with an opportunity to tell his or her side of the story; this is not a cross-examination, but a final chance for the employee to give an explanation for what appears to be poor behaviour or unsatisfactory performance; and
   - the investigation interview should be separated from the subsequent disciplinary interview, when the employee is advised of the corrective action — there should be at least a ten minute break, time to get a coffee or some other kind of pause; sometimes the break will be longer, but it should not be any longer than a couple of days.
2. In some cases, it is appropriate to suspend an employee pending investigation. If you determine that an employee should not be present in the workplace because of a serious incident, but you have not had time to complete a suitable investigation, you may tell an employee not to attend work in the meantime. Depending on the circumstances, this suspension could be with or without pay. In most cases, it should be for a period of only a few days. Some cases have featured much longer suspensions pending investigation, especially if there is a serious incident that involves public trust.

3. In most cases, you should aim to complete your investigation and determine the extent of corrective action, if any, within a week of the incident or circumstances giving rise to the investigation.

Mitigating Circumstances:
Fitting Corrective Action to the Misconduct

The severity of the misconduct, misbehaviour or poor performance of an employee will have a significant impact on the level of corrective action that is assessed. Breaching safety rules, assault or the intentional destruction of the employer's property are considered to be more serious acts of misconduct than lateness, and, for that reason alone, would tend to result in more severe corrective action. Several other mitigating or extenuating factors should be considered before settling on appropriate corrective action, such as:

- seniority or length of service;
- problems away from the workplace;
- the potential for rehabilitation, which may be established largely by the employee's reaction to the investigation process and his or her willingness to accept responsibility;
- provocation by other employees or other circumstances that contributed to the situation;
- an apparent need for additional training;
- concerns about flaws in the investigation process itself; and
- most important, the prior record of corrective action that has been taken in respect of this employee; on this final factor, there are at least four points to keep in mind:
  - although you may decide to separate out certain performance issues and deal with them on their own — attendance management being the most obvious — there is no need in general to have different streams of corrective action to deal with different categories of misconduct; you should have one main stream of corrective action in which past misconduct of any category is relevant to the present determination;
  - as a counter-balance to the point above, the more recent and the more similar the prior corrective action, the more significant should be its impact on the current situation;
  - at some point, prior corrective action should become stale, unless it deals with the most serious of offences; generally

speaking, two years is a suitable time frame, so that if an employee does not engage in misconduct during that period, then prior corrective action should be removed from the record or at least declared to be stale;

- one of the important aspects of corrective action that is progressive is that even relatively minor misconduct could lead to a dismissal if there is a significant record of prior and reasonably current corrective action; in common parlance, this is known as the straw that broke the camel's back or the brick that bent the axle; in labour relations, this is referred to as dismissal based on a culminating incident.

Once you have taken corrective action, you should not take other or more severe corrective action for the same incident of misconduct. You should be sure to explain this clearly to your front-line supervisors. If, for example, they are faced with a disruptive or inebriated employee on an afternoon or night shift, the proper action is to send the employee home without pay pending investigation. Many supervisors have made the mistake of telling the employee that s/he is suspended for the balance of the shift, which fixes the corrective action. If it is subsequently determined that the employee has a record of corrective action and should have been dismissed, the argument of cause for dismissal may have been compromised by the supervisor's initial announcement. This trap for unwary employers sometimes takes on the name of the equivalent concept in criminal law: "double jeopardy".

Sometimes new or additional facts are obtained after the imposition of the discipline, which may lead to having the penalty reassessed. In such cases, if you hope to succeed in court with an argument of cause for dismissal and avoid a claim of double jeopardy, then you should be able to show that the new or additional facts could not have been determined in the course of a reasonable investigation prior to the original corrective action.

Summary of an Effective CAP

- Ensure that your employees are informed of the rules and standards to which they must conform.
- Enforce these rules and standards in a consistent and equitable fashion.
- React in a timely manner to all breaches of the rules and standards.
- Thoroughly investigate incidents of misconduct and ensure that the employee who is alleged to have engaged in the misconduct receives a full and fair opportunity to provide you with an explanation.
- Act promptly, especially in serious cases and/or if you have suspended an employee pending investigation.
- Base your decision as to the appropriate corrective action on all the facts and circumstances of the current situation. Remember to give careful consideration to possible mitigating or extenuating circumstances and to the record.
- Discuss with the employee the action that you are taking in the privacy of your office, preferably with another management witness in attendance.
- Create a written record, except for cases of preliminary oral counselling, where it may suffice for you to write a note to yourself.
- Follow up on corrective action. Take further action if it is warranted or let an employee know that his/her performance is improving.
- Make sure that supervisors and managers consult with the HRP to review the proposed corrective action and to comment on the letter or form; also ensure that the decision-maker has the required authority to take action.

The Final Break from Employment — A Review of Dismissal Scenarios

It is increasingly rare that people retire from the company or organization where they first had full-time employment. For employees at all levels, and especially at higher levels, it is normal to change jobs, perhaps many times over the 40 or 50 years that is a typical adult work span. There are many reasons why an employee would leave employment, and these were summarized in chapter 2 above, which dealt with the common law of contracts as it applies to employment. This review will focus on the three key types of employer-initiated dismissals in which work performance is the issue.

Disciplinary Discharge or Dismissal for Cause

Whether or not you use the CAP, or something similar to it, you may have a situation in which an employee's misconduct (either a single incident or a series of incidents of sub-standard behaviour) is so significant that it shatters any prospect for a viable employment relationship. Trust is gone. Workplace relationships are poisoned. The very presence of the employee in the workplace is worse than neutral, it is detrimental to the performance of other employees, and of the overall group.

Sometimes old words perfectly capture the sense of a situation. Here, the word is <u>moribund</u>. By the action or actions of the employee, the employee relationship is essentially dead. The problem is proving cause, especially if you have not used a CAP, or if the facts of the single or final incident are in dispute, or if the significance of the misconduct is challenged.

Dismissal for Poor Performance, but Not for Cause

Cause is very difficult to prove, although effective use of a CAP will help greatly. With the danger of *Wallace* damages lurking behind every case in which cause is put into play by the employer (see chapter 2 above), and with the increased time and expense that would accompany any case in which cause is disputed, many employers opt simply to pay off an employee who has sub-standard performance. As well, many employers do not have the time or patience to fully implement a CAP or other progressive system.

Subject to statutory restrictions, like human rights considerations, an employer can terminate any employee at any time. The usual question is not whether it can be done, but how much will it cost? In other words, and as previously noted, it is not the dismissal that is wrongful — the dispute in a wrongful dismissal case is all about the amount that is paid in lieu of notice. When terminating employment due to poor performance, but not for cause, there are at least three points to keep in focus:

- Once you have made the decision to dismiss the employee, it should be all business. Especially in view of *Wallace*, you should be sensible, sensitive, and civilized in handling the termination interview, the settlement offer, as well as the physical exit from the workplace premises. This is not the time for parting shots.
- While you should be as diplomatic and professional as possible, you should continue to be upfront about the reason for dismissal, especially in cases where a human rights complaint is a realistic possibility. If poor performance is the issue, you should say so, and make any settlement offer without prejudice to that view. The danger otherwise is that you could find yourself on the wrong side of a case in which the employee claims that the dismissal was due to the exercise of statutory rights (such as making a complaint under human rights or health and safety legislation). If you have already given some banal, feel-good reason for the termination, it is likely too late to argue that the real reason was, after all, performance.
- Once you have made the decision not to terminate for cause, subject to legal wrangling that may follow the rejection of an offer of settlement that is made without prejudice, performance is no longer a factor in determining the amount that is owing to an employee. Whether terminated due to economic circumstances or his or her own performance, if the employer is not prepared to assert cause, then the employee is entitled to the full range of damages for the dismissal.

Dismissal for Non-Performance: Non-Disciplinary Absenteeism

The issue of absenteeism and its consequences for an employment relationship was introduced in chapter 3 above, dealing with performance management. That section provides further details about how to proceed with a dismissal in those kinds of situations. If done correctly, such dismissals stand a reasonable chance of succeeding without giving rise to a legitimate claim for damages. As with many employment situations, but especially because these are dismissals that have human rights and possibly other statutory implications, you probably should get legal advice from the outset, or at least before taking the final action.

If an employee is ill or injured and absent from the workplace for an indefinite period, there comes a time when the employer can fairly conclude that there is no reasonable expectation that the employee will be able to resume employment, even if the work is modified to accommodate medical restrictions. It is typical to wait two years before making such a determination. The period of time may vary according to disability plans and workers' compensation situations if you are dealing with a compensable situation.

For most cases, there is a two-step dismissal process:

- Make sure that you get current medical information. Let the employee know, by letter, what medical information you have on file, and that the information indicates that the employee is unable to return to work. Invite the employee to provide further or different medical information. Make clear to the employee that, unless there is information that indicates the realistic possibility of a return in the foreseeable future, then employment will be terminated. Clarify the status of any disability coverage. Provide the employee with a timeframe for response, typically two weeks and indicate that, if no response, you will assume that your information is correct.

- Act promptly on whatever response you get, including a failure to respond within the time frame. If the information suggests that employment may resume in the near future, then you should become very active on the file, to ensure that you are not simply being placed into an indefinite holding pattern. Insist on dates for further medical reports, within weeks, not months, and consider getting an independent medical review or even an independent medical examination if you have concerns about the quality of the medical reporting.

The other kind of non-performance due to absenteeism is when an employee is frequently absent for short periods. Dealing with this kind of absenteeism becomes complicated if some of the absences are due to workplace injuries or illnesses. As well, Ontario's emergency leave provisions, introduced in September 2001, effectively provide employees with a free ride for up to ten days per year. That said, for most cases, there is a three-step dismissal process, with each step featuring a meeting and a follow-up letter:

1. Introduce the problem, with statistics going back a year or two. You will need good attendance records, and you should relate the employee to his or her own group (such as a production unit or an office unit). Indicate that the employee's attendance is below the norm. Clarify that this is not disciplinary — you are not challenging the reasons for absence. Recommend that the employee get medical assistance to deal with any underlying problems. Provide the employee with a timeframe for improvement, typically two or three months. Warn that failure to improve attendance could lead to dismissal. Follow up with the employee at the end of that period or in the meantime, if the problem continues to be serious.

2. Follow up. If the problem is the same or worse, then you should provide a final monitoring period of the same length (two or three months). Make it as clear as possible that a failure to improve attendance likely will result in dismissal.

3. Dismiss or follow up for the final time at the end of the second monitoring period. In some cases, you might give one last chance to an employee. A proper exercise of managerial discretion requires that each case be considered on its own merits. If an employee appears to be making a real effort to improve attendance, then you should be patient. As with progressive discipline, when you are dealing with a situation of frequent short-term absenteeism, the goal is to improve the employee's attendance, not to terminate employment.

An employment relationship is a bargain between the employee and the employer. If the employer is no longer getting the full benefit of the bargain, then the employer should take action. The nature of the action that should be taken depends on a proper analysis of the problem. The point is that there is always some action that could be taken, whether the problem is one of attitude, ability or absenteeism.

◆

CHAPTER 7

ENCOURAGING SUGGESTIONS AND COMPLAINTS

There are no perfect workplaces. Every workplace is dynamic. Every workplace is full of challenges. Even the most positive workplaces will not have everyone headed in the same direction all the time. When there is conflict in the workplace between management and workers, there must be an avenue available to workers to bring forward complaints or concerns. Workers expect to be heard. If they have a valid basis for complaint, workers expect an effective and prompt remedy. If they are unsuccessful at first, workers expect at least a second level reconsideration of their complaint.

With an effective complaints procedure, management will find out about problems that were unknown or under-appreciated. In most cases, management will have the opportunity to intervene with solutions that are not costly and actually may benefit the organization. Mistakes can be corrected before any real damage is done. Opportunities can be realized before it is too late to gain the full benefit of a good idea.

Complaints are Normal

One of the key responsibilities of management is to detect and, where possible, prevent problems or disputes from escalating into full-blown disputes. As is so often the case in matters of human resources management, the spotlight is on the front-line supervisor, who deals with the employees on a day-to-day basis. This is an especially important responsibility for supervisors in a non-union workplace, because unattended discontent creates fertile ground for union organizing campaigns.

The best supervisors cannot avoid disputes or prevent complaints. Indeed, it is often very good supervisors who cause complaints because of their insistence on high standards of behaviour or performance. Anyone with teenage children would recognize that setting expectations and insisting on compliance is not always a path strewn with flowers. In many cases dealing with some of your workers likely will not be much different.

There is nothing wrong with complaints. Think of them as just another way for employees to make suggestions about how the workplace should be managed. Not only will complaints alert the management team to potential problems, they are also a good way for employees to let off steam. While you do not want to encourage negativism and conflict in your workplace, you certainly should make it easy for employees to complain and to have their complaints resolved. Indeed, if you think of complaints as suggestions, then approach the project of creating a complaint procedure as an evolution of the suggestion box.

Opening the Door:
a Real Procedure for Suggestions and Complaints

In a union workplace, a formal grievance procedure is a legal requirement. At the end of the procedure, it is open to either party (typically the union) to submit any unresolved dispute to binding arbitration by a neutral adjudicator. If you are in a non-union workplace, you should want to minimize this obvious union sales pitch while gaining the advantages of the evolved suggestion box. Your objective should be to create an effective vehicle for your employees to have their complaints registered and considered.

In my view, it is insufficient to say that you have an "open-door" policy. Often, your view that you have an open door may be nothing more than a vague hope that you are approachable. Your employees may have a much different perception. They may be shy and without self-confidence. They may have difficulty articulating their views and concerns. They may be afraid that complaints will diminish their standing in the workplace and affect their job security and opportunity for advancement. If you really do have an open door policy that employees feel comfortable walking through, then you should have no difficulty making sure that open door is completely transparent and accessible to all.

Even the best open-door manager will fall short of a union grievance procedure. That is because open-door managers expect one-stop shopping. They expect that either they will be able to resolve the worker's issue or convince the worker that s/he has no real issue. By contrast, every grievance procedure features at least a second step and often a third or fourth step. These additional steps allow the employee to have an initial decision reconsidered at progressively higher levels of managerial authority.

If you were to follow the model of a standard grievance procedure, this is how your non-union procedure for suggestions and complaints might look:

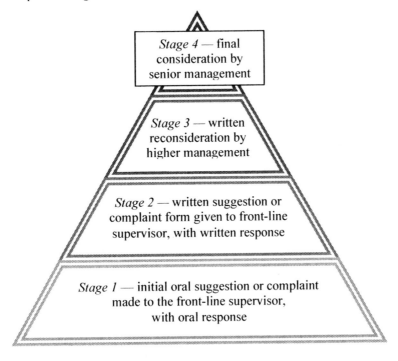

Stage 4 — final consideration by senior management

Stage 3 — written reconsideration by higher management

Stage 2 — written suggestion or complaint form given to front-line supervisor, with written response

Stage 1 — initial oral suggestion or complaint made to the front-line supervisor, with oral response

Details of a Suggestion and Complaint Procedure

If you add some time frames and provide employees with a form that is easy to use, then the only thing that would differentiate your non-union procedure for suggestions and complaints from its union counterpart (the grievance procedure) would be the lack of an arbitration procedure following the final stage. An arbitration hearing is a reasonably formal legal proceeding, in which the parties are the employer and the union, acting on its own behalf or on behalf of an employee. The arbitrator is typically a lawyer or a professional with experience and training in mediation and arbitration. The arbitrator is unbiased and neutral, and has no relationship with either party. In most cases, the arbitrator issues a written decision, often with detailed reasons. To a very limited extent, an arbitrator's decision could be reviewed in court, but generally, as a matter of fact and law, arbitral decisions are final and binding on the parties, and set a precedent for similar disputes between the two parties in question.

Trying to come up with a substitute for the arbitration process is the biggest challenge for non-union workplaces. It is not impossible, but it may be too awkward to attempt. At the very least, if you understand that a comparable union procedure would have arbitration as the final stage, then it will become all the more important for you to make sure that your procedure for suggestions and complaints really works.

Let us look a little more closely at each of the three points raised above: time frames, a form, and a substitute for arbitration:

1. *Time Frames*: Suggestions or complaints should be made when they actually arise or soon thereafter — a matter of days at most. In the same way, the initial response should be right away or within a couple of days. It should be stressed that it is absolutely essential that there be some response. There is no excuse for a failure to respond. If a supervisor needs more information, then the employee should be advised of that and a response should be forthcoming as soon as the information is obtained. Each of the subsequent steps should take place within days, or at most a couple of weeks (especially at higher steps, where meetings may be scheduled). It is always the same process: the employee makes or advances the complaint, management considers it at each level, and then management makes a response.

2. *Suggestion and Complaint Form*: Even without a formal system, most complaints originate in an informal manner and are made orally. A formal system should provide employees with the opportunity to make a formal written complaint if the informal complaint does not lead to a prompt resolution. A complaint form creates simplicity for the employees and consistency for management, which makes the complaint process both easy to use and more likely to be effective. Here is a sample form:

[Employer logo]

EMPLOYEE SUGGESTION & COMPLAINT FORM

Name of employee: _____   *Date:*_____

*Description of suggestion or complaint:*_____

_____

_____

*Applicable standard(s) or rule(s):*_____

_____

_____

*Action or remedy requested:*_____

_____

_____

*Response by the Employer, with reasons:*_____

_____

_____

*Signature of Supervisor/Manager:*_____*Date:*_____

*Name and Position of Supervisor/Manager:*_____

I have received and read this response:_____

Employee's Signature

I am satisfied _____ *OR I wish to have my complaint considered at a higher level*

---

3. *Substitute for Arbitration:* At the very least, there are two practices that can go a long way. First, senior management should be involved at the final step. This could be the HRP, if considered to be a senior position within the operation, or a senior operations manager, such as a plant manager in a manufacturing facility. Second, at the final step, and perhaps the final couple of steps, there should be a meeting where an employee has an opportunity to present the issue.

103

There are two other practices that should be considered:

- the workers could be allowed to appoint one or more worker advocates, who would take the role of a union steward — these advocates could be permanent appointments, for all workers, or individually selected by a worker on a case by case basis, and their use would be entirely at the option of the worker; and
- a neutral mediator could be appointed as a final step, beyond the highest level of management; however, true neutrality would be compromised to some extent by the fact that the employer would foot the bill, and the employer would probably want to limit the authority of the mediator to implement only resolutions that are mutually accepted, both by the employer and the affected worker(s).

As an alternative to this last practice, I have seen worker review boards (peer review) used with some success to reconsider corrective action, but that is not a practice I recommend.

A Closer Look at the Steps of the Procedure

Suggestions or complaints may deal with the following issues or situations:

- the improper interpretation, application or general administration of different aspects of the framework;
- improper classification, in that the worker claims to be doing a different kind of work than that for which s/he is being paid;
- unjust discipline, especially if unpaid suspension or dismissal.

Even if you have a comprehensive framework and a classification system that is both reasonable and well communicated, these are written in English. The English language is incapable of capturing all of the factual permutations and combinations that can arise with human interactions in a workplace. Indeed, management does not want a framework that is so clear and so detailed that there is no room for the exercise of discretion. If you take the flexibility out of a workplace, it becomes brittle and fragile. In any event, you cannot anticipate all issues and disputes that may arise in the time period following the creation or renewal of a framework. Complaints and disputes are inevitable. Employees are bound to think that they have a better way to do things, and maybe they do. An effective suggestion and complaint procedure acts as a problem-solving mechanism and should lead to the calm, rational and open resolution of workplace discontent.

To return to a consistent theme, the front-line supervisor plays a key role in the early steps of the suggestion and complaint procedure. In the later stages, the process usually becomes more formal and the involvement of senior management and human resources becomes more prominent. Since the front-line supervisor usually has the best information about the circumstances of the complaint, s/he should remain involved throughout the process, even though the ultimate decision may be made at a higher level within the management team.

Nowhere is the front-line supervisor more important than at the initial oral complaint stage. If you are enthusiastic about setting up a procedure, do not get carried away. Do not take away the essential informality that should exist at the very beginning. The requirement that all complaints and suggestions be raised directly with the front-line supervisor in the normal course of day-to-day communications remains an integral first step in the process. This step provides an opportunity for the supervisor and employee to resolve the problem quickly and with the least amount of fuss.

At this initial stage, neither a complaint nor the response is written. Since the intention is to have the complaint expressed orally and informally, do not expect a bright light to shine or a red arrow to appear over an employee's head to indicate that the complaint process has been initiated. The rule for a supervisor is that whenever an employee brings a suggestion of complaint to his or her attention or questions an action, this suggestion and complaint procedure has been activated and the supervisor should respond, orally and promptly, in the required manner. The supervisor should make a brief note of any such situation, always following the W5 rule — who, what, why, when and where.

Front-line supervisors who have open communications with their workers may be able to get a tremendous amount of unfiltered information at the initial stage of a suggestion or complaint. If the situation passes on to more formal stages of the procedure, workers may get locked into positions that are no longer truly reflective of the original concern. Listen carefully at the outset and you may find a solution that, even if not originally accepted, can be resurrected at a later stage.

Responses and Resolutions to
Suggestions and Complaints

A front-line supervisor may have limited authority to resolve issues that are raised in suggestions and complaints, either at the initial oral stage or at the second stage, when a written complaint is filed. Even so, the supervisor should bear the primary responsibility for the initial investigation and the first responses, both orally and in writing. Naturally, the supervisor is part of the management team and should seek guidance and support from colleagues, superiors and the HRP in all but the most obvious cases.

If higher-level management becomes involved at later stages, they have to achieve a balance between trying to find a resolution that is satisfactory to everyone and trying to avoid contradicting or undercutting the authority of the front-line supervisor. Some of this balance can be achieved ahead of time by educating supervisors, especially if a worker has been subjected to corrective action. Supervisors have to understand that, while their decisions will be considered carefully and always respected, compromises may take place. Indeed, at the early stages of the procedure, supervisors themselves may be prepared to fashion compromises. At later stages, supervisors should be encouraged to participate in trying to find an effective compromise.

It is hard to have an effective procedure for suggestions and complaints from workers if the answer is always "no". Sometimes, "no" is the only appropriate answer. To determine what the answer should be in any particular situation, here are some guidelines:

- Do not jump to conclusions. Wait until you have all the facts and circumstances behind the suggestion or complaint before responding.
- Settle the issue on its merits. Provide the worker with his/her entitlement under the framework. When the facts and circumstances fully support management's actions, say "no". On the other hand, admit mistakes graciously and grant an appropriate remedy. Whatever you decide, provide a reasonable explanation of the reasons for your decision to the employee.
- If you deny any remedy or benefit to the worker or you reject a suggestion, the written response should be fairly simple and straightforward. Depending on the nature of the issue the

response could reinforce the framework or confirm the appropriateness of a position classification, performance appraisal or corrective action.

- If your complaint procedure has time guidelines, or if there is a limited period of time for receiving suggestions in respect of a particular issue, and the worker does not adhere to the guidelines, it may be appropriate to refuse to consider the complaint or suggestion. Management could be flexible in this respect, but you should always make clear to a worker when a complaint or suggestion is untimely.
- Carefully consider the implications of any settlement. Even if you ensure that it has no legal effect, this employee and other workers could still view it as an indication of how management will act in response to similar situations in the future. As a general rule, you should avoid "nuisance" settlements, as they only encourage frivolous complaints. If senior management settles on this basis, they are often completely undercutting the supervisor, thereby turning a minor issue into a major problem within the management team. By "nuisance" settlement, I mean those situations where the employee has no basis for a claim, but it is such a minor cost that you give the employee what s/he has asked for.
- If you are prepared to provide the employee with some benefit or remedy as a result of the suggestion or complaint, you should get a written settlement, either as a separate document, or as a sign-back from the employee of your response. If you use a form, you could achieve the settlement on the form itself. Here are important elements of any written settlement:
  - identify the suggestion or complaint in question;
  - indicate that the parties have reached a settlement;
  - clearly state the terms of the settlement;
  - stipulate that the worker is satisfied that there has been a complete resolution;
  - where appropriate (it could be overkill in many cases), you may wish to indicate that the settlement is without admission of liability, is without prejudice and does not constitute a precedent for other employees; this means that the settlement could not be introduced in a subsequent legal proceeding as evidence of the employer's view as to its legal position in this situation or a similar situation;

- carefully consider the implications and impact of a proposed settlement.

Here is a review of some important features in avoiding unnecessary complaints:

- Communicate with your workers. Do not be reluctant to explain your actions or your planned changes to your people.
- If a worker tells you about a problem or complaint, ensure that s/he is kept informed of what you are doing about it. A worker will often be patient so long as s/he knows that the problem is being considered, not ignored.
- Listen carefully and between the lines. If a problem seems trivial, try to understand what is the real basis for the complaint.
- Act promptly to deal with the complaint, but avoid making snap judgments. Impulsive actions or statements often lead to mistakes. However, unjustified delay likely will frustrate the employee and could make a simple issue more serious.
- Avoid creating an atmosphere where employees feel that the only way to obtain consideration of their problems is through the written stages of the procedure.
- Treat each situation as unique. No two problems are completely identical and, therefore, identical solutions may not be appropriate. Supervisors should get any necessary approvals before indicating or promising anything to the employee.
- Do not make commitments or promises that you cannot keep. Do not raise expectations that cannot be met.
- Admit your mistakes and correct them as soon as you are aware that an error has been made. Covering up or trying to circumvent the framework will only damage your reputation with your employees. Your employees' respect and trust in your integrity will increase when they realize that you readily admit mistakes but stand firm when you are right.
- Provide the employees with their entitlement under the framework. Apply the framework in a consistent, reasonable and unbiased manner.

Proactive Steps to Avoid Unnecessary Complaints

As mentioned earlier, the front-line supervisor is responsible for attempting to detect and resolve problems at the earliest possible opportunity. A concerted effort to avoid unnecessary complaints should not compromise any of management's rights. In fact, listening to your employees and trying to resolve problems before they actually materialize incorporates sound management principles and should enhance the effectiveness of the management team.

◆

CHAPTER 8

RENEWAL AND CHANGE

Change is inevitable. The old joke about life is that the one who has the most at the end wins. While some religions and philosophies suggest that there is a state of perfect balance that might be achievable in this lifetime, the next one, or some other one, I am unaware of a state of perfect harmony for an organization. The only state of existence for an organization that seems certain is that it will be different tomorrow than it is today. Unlike the joke, the workplace is not a race to the end, it is an ongoing process.

You Never Actually Get There

On my fridge is a magnet with a saying that will be common to most of you, "life is a journey, not a destination". That is certainly true for most organizations. Unless they are set up for a limited purpose or for a limited period of time, most organizations have an indefinite existence. For most of us, life within our workplaces is an ongoing journey. We never actually arrive. The best that we can hope for, especially in terms of human resources management, is to get close to where we want to be. If you think you are where you want to be, you are likely delusional or entirely without ambition. I doubt that you will be reading this book, or, if you started, you will not have bothered to get this far.

Whether we are far away, very close to where we want to be or, by miracle or illusion, finally there, it is not a fixed state. You will have to keep changing or change will keep happening to you. Your destination, assuming that you can define an ideal framework for human resources management with reasonable accuracy, is a moving target. If you ever get close, you will have to keep moving to stay close. Indeed, you will likely find that something that got you close, or at least moved you ahead at one time in the evolution of your organization, is no longer valid or helpful.

Once you accept that constant evolution is innately human and as much a part of our organizations as it is of our individual selves, then you should have no problem adopting the notion that continuous renewal is not only necessary, it should be an integral part of your human resources framework. You should plan for change. You should lead change. Whatever is bad in your workplace can be made less so. Whatever is good can be made better. Whatever is excellent must be nourished and reinforced constantly. Indeed, you want to ride the crest of excellence in one area of your workplace to improve other areas that lag behind.

The Calendar System

Your framework will have key elements, depending on the nature of your workplace. Every framework should have safety and human rights as two of the elements; indeed, human rights could be divided further into discrimination (especially in terms of persons with disabilities) and harassment (especially sexual or racial harassment). Other key elements may include attendance, individual performance evaluation — featuring quality of production or service, and training in maintaining skills and acquiring new skills.

I suggest that you start with four or five key elements and stop at eight or nine. Assign a month to each of the elements. Avoid the month of your fiscal year end. Avoid December and avoid your two or three primary vacation months (typically the summer).

In each assigned month, every year, you will do the following:

- review and revise the relevant parts of the framework, including any policies, procedures, rules or practices that might apply, as well as any materials that may have been produced, such as employee booklets or an actual phantom collective agreement if you have one;
- in the course of your review, you should seek input from all employees, as discussed in chapter 4 above;
- communicate the key aspects of the element in question and conduct training, first of the management team and then of your workers and other employees; and
- complete any related tasks, such as performance evaluations in your quality month or a comprehensive safety inspection in safety month.

Paradigms for Learning

Whether you are the trainer or you are being trained yourself, it is important to focus on using the information to achieve a positive change in management practices. You should engage in training with a clear approach in mind for giving or receiving the information in a manner that will allow it to be put to practical use in the workplace.

There are two approaches to learning that you are encouraged to consider as an appropriate framework for the materials I have presented in this book. The first approach is called VISION; the second is called LEADER. Here is each one in summary form:

VISION	LEADER
Visualize	Leadership
Internalize	Excellence
Scrutinize	Action
Inform	Documentation
Organize	Evidence
Normalize — Now Go Do It!	Responsibility

The two approaches work together and should be viewed as two different angles on improving your human resources management and maintaining a non-union workplace. You may well come up with your own approaches. Indeed, it is a good exercise, as you read these materials, to try to develop your own personal framework that you can use afterwards to guide you in implementing effective workplace practices.

VISION

VISION is a collection of ideas that you should find applicable in any training situation, whether you are giving the training or receiving it, and whether the training consists of reading a book or listening to an oral presentation. The point of VISION is to access the materials in a direct and personal way. This may be a book that is written by Jamie Knight, but it is also a book that is read by each of you. As soon as you start reading my book, it becomes your book. Each of you will have a different experience with the book, depending on your own background, as well as the energy and intelligence that you put into reading the ideas contained in these pages.

If the ideas in my book are to be effective in your workplace, then you have to transform my ideas into your ideas. In other words, VISION is not mine, it is meant to be yours.

- *Visualize:* As you read these materials, try to think about situations within your experience or imagination that relate to what you are reading. Translate the best of what is in these pages into training exercises, where you can create case studies out of the concepts that you are learning about.
- *Internalize:* As you read and visualize situations to which you can relate, try to make your own sense of what you are reading. Make connections between the concepts in these pages and your own knowledge and experience. Whether or not you are experienced in human resources management, you likely have a significant set of skills that is unique and certainly valuable. These pages are not meant to create something out of nothing; rather they should challenge, shape and augment the knowledge that is already part of you.
- *Scrutinize:* There is no single source of all knowledge. You will not find all of the answers in one place. It is rare, if it ever happens, that you will read something or listen to something and accept all of it as right and good. Read critically. Make sure that what you are reading makes sense for you and your organization. Most importantly, if it does not make sense, do not simply be dismissive — that is too easy and lazy. Come up with your own better answer and connect it with other concepts that make better sense.
- *Inform:* Inform yourself and inform others. You should not read this book in one sitting. Indeed, you probably should not even read it from front to back. Scribble all over it. Highlight it. Underline it. Most importantly, discuss it, with your colleagues, with your superiors, and even with the people whom you supervise. Human resources management is not a solitary pursuit. Do not try to learn in isolation.

- *Organize:* As you visualize, internalize, scrutinize and inform yourself and others about these ideas and your own related ideas, organize all of this knowledge so that you can make sense of it and apply it. Patterns and systems for organization have been suggested throughout these materials, including VISION and LEADER. Feel free to create and use your own patterns and systems. Once you are done with this book, you should not be lost in a mess of new ideas. Rather, you should have a system, based on your prior knowledge and experience, which will allow you to manage people at your workplace even better than before.

- *Normalize:* With a system in place, you should be able to put some new ideas into action. Never try to do everything at once. Whole-scale changes in human resources management practices are generally counter-productive and even dangerous. Significant change is a key indicator of an organization that could be ripe for union organizing activity. Effective change is usually incremental and easy to digest by the affected workplace players. Pick two or three of the best ideas that come out of reading this book. Put those ideas into place in an organized and staged manner. Do not wait for a better idea to come along; as soon as you have a couple of good ideas, get to work. If the first changes are successful, and when you feel that your organization is ready for more change, pick the next two or three ideas and implement those. Not everything is going to work, but most should.

These changes are like plants — you cannot just pop the seed into the ground and hope for the best. You have to nurture the change and make it part of your normal workplace environment. Indeed, even when the change has firmly taken root, you have to revisit it from time to time to make sure that it is still healthy and not choked off by the weeds of ignorance and apathy.

LEADER

Although this book makes frequent reference to the <u>management</u> of human resources, it is also a key recommendation of the book that you should aspire to <u>leadership</u>. For our purposes, leadership is not meant to be a more highly developed form of management. The two act together. Leadership without management would be chaos. It would be like the meetings that too many of us attend where there are fantastic and creative ideas, but no action is ever taken.

Management without leadership is at best merely adequate and at worst without purpose. We all have to put out fires in our workplaces, often on a daily basis. If you spend all of your time putting out fires, then you are simply coping — you are not going anywhere. There is no point in being organized and efficient if you have no direction. It is for that reason that the word efficient always should be joined with the word effective — do it well, but do it with a clear objective in mind. Another coupling to remember is that it is important to be reactive (management), but you must also be proactive (leadership).

- *Leadership:* Do not simply manage. Learn from yesterday. Plan for tomorrow. Act today. This is your workplace. You are part of the brain of the employer. Where do you want to take the workplace today and in the years to come?
- *Excellence:* This is your workplace. You set the standards. Set your standards high. Excellence should be your goal, not just good enough.
- *Action:* Do something! Most mistakes in human resources management and in leading people happen because nothing was done when something should have been done. There are usually different things that could be done. Within reason, any one of those possibilities is probably better than doing nothing at all. If you keep sweeping everything under the rug, then eventually the rug is going to smell bad. If you keep running away from confrontation, then you will soon run away from your job as well.
- *Documentation:* Cover your assets — yours and the organization that employs you. Make notes of any interesting situations that occur in your workplace. Make more structured reports when warranted by particular situations. Use formal communication systems when you have something formal to communicate, like discipline or policies or standard operating procedures. Make life easier. Develop forms for the most common kinds of written communications. Follow a standard reporting system — W5: who, what, why, when and where. Usually you should have recommendations to make; otherwise, keep your reports factual — leave your opinions out of them. With practice and a consistent system, you will

find that you can make a decent initial note very quickly, often in a minute or two.

- *Evidence:* Preserve the present. If there are items that relate to a situation (a tool or scrap product perhaps), then you should consider hanging on to those items until the situation is fully resolved. Take photographs or videos. Use diagrams — even your own bad scratching will be much better than nothing at all. Use existing blueprints or schematics if relevant.

- *Responsibility:* Pass the buck if you do not have the full or final authority to take action in any particular situation. But always pass the buck with value added. You are not simply a messenger if you are part of the management team. You are part of the management brain. You are expected to contribute to decision-making even if the final decision is not yours. Manage your own boss by giving your boss all of the information that he or she requires in order to make the decision that you think is best.

Continuous Improvement

Throughout the pages of this book, you have been encouraged to manage the situations that arise in your workplace in a manner that is efficient and that solves problems. You also have been challenged to look for opportunities to lead your workplace. You should feel empowered to seek out and be at the forefront of continuous improvement in your workplace. Continuous improvement in human resources management will make your workplace more effective and more productive. It also should make your workplace less vulnerable to union organizing activity.

Continuous improvement is not simply a catchy concept; it should be an objective at the heart of any organization. Whatever you are doing today, and however well you are doing it, you could be doing it better tomorrow. To do it better, you may have to make significant changes. Effective and long-lasting change takes time to implement, so you had better get busy with changes that make sense for your workplace, and stay busy throughout your career.

Index

Absenteeism *See also* **Dismissal situations**
blameless absenteeism, 47-48
   long-term illnesses or injuries, 47
   short-term absences, repetitive, 47-48
culpable absenteeism, 47
dismissal for non-performance: non-disciplinary absenteeism, 95-97
   long-term illness or injuries, 96
     dismissal process, two-step, 96
      medical information, obtaining current, 96
      prompt action on employee response to information
        request, 96
   generally, 95-96
   short-term absences, repetitive, 97
     dismissal process, three-step, 97
      dismissal or follow up, 97
      follow up and monitoring period, 97
      informing and warning, 97
generally, 87

"At will" employment
   American concept, 19
   Canadian equivalency with clear written contract, 19
   legal protection, some, 19
   presumption, 18

Boundaries of human resources management
common law boundary, 15-25
   components, three significant, 15-16
   generally, 15-16
   law of contracts, 15, 16-19
     "at will" employment, 18-19
      American concept, 19
      Canadian equivalency with clear written contract, 19
      legal protection, some, 19
      presumption, 18

119